S0-AAD-542

➤ LOOKING FORWARD
The Journal of the Aspen Center for Social Values

A quarterly journal, which features thought-provoking articles that stimulate debate and propose solutions to important social issues around the world.

Ira Bedzow Editor-in-Chief
Mark Goldfeder Managing Editor
Malka Fleischmann Associate Editor
Jason Koslowe Associate Editor
Ilene Goldfeder Art Direction

The Aspen Center for Social Values is more than a think tank. It is a network of socially-minded individuals seeking practical ideas to solve pressing social challenges. Its mission is to leverage the unique assets of the Jewish tradition to promote serious thought about - and to bring a fresh and unique voice to - social and societal challenges that confront the world today.

The Center's important work is made possible through the support of its members and contributors. Please visit our website - www.theaspencenter.org - and join our community.

The Aspen Center for Social Values
435 West Main Street
Aspen, CO 81611
Tel. 970-544-3770

➤ LOOKING FORWARD
The Journal of the Aspen Center for Social Values

Submission of Articles

If you would like to submit an article to Looking Forward, please send us a short description of the essay you would like to write at Looking.Forward@theaspencenter.org. Articles should be about something that is timely and relevant to our readership. Opinions on current events, analyses of recent research or findings, or prescriptive articles regarding a contemporary issue or problem would be appropriate.

Looking Forward welcomes letters to the Editor. If you would like to send us a letter, please email Looking.Forward@theaspencenter.org.

Advertising in the Journal

If you would like to advertise in Looking Forward, please send an email at Looking.Forward@theaspencenter.org.

Looking Forward will be published four times per year in January, March, June, and September.

We would like to thank the Looking Forward Editorial Board as well as the anonymous reviewers – who range from academics, clergy members, and lay leaders - for all their help reviewing and improving the articles. Without them, the journal would not be at the high level of quality that it is.

➤ Table of Contents

THE ASPEN CENTER FOR SOCIAL VALUES
Addressing Social Values through Thought and Action

➤ Introduction

their actions and in their capacity to convince others to share their vision. In this landmark issue are the words of true Jewish leaders who demand that no one be left a bystander.

Our issue begins with a fresh look at the Pew study findings, the analysis of which suggests where opportunities lie for the Jewish community at large, allowing us to confront the challenges raised in the report. We continue with pieces from leaders that urge us to leave our comfort zones and act – to start moving towards a different future. Yet action, as other leaders note, can only take a person so far; it is necessary to deepen its effects by deepening its meaning. Knowledge – i.e. an understanding of how our tradition and history lend significance to our practices – will merge Jewish action and Jewish identity.

Complementing the idealism that leads all of us forward, our leaders also recognize the pressures and struggles that exist when individuals move together, each at his or her own pace. No one should gain at the moral expense of others, and everyone should be held responsible for protecting each other. Theological duty does not whitewash interpersonal offense, and social action does not replace religious humility. There must be institutional and communal safeguards to ensure that people can feel safe in trusting those who guide us. Still others discuss the power of education, both at an institutional level and as a personal value. The education of our future leaders depends on the opportunities we provide them today, and the recognition of that chain of transmission and our responsibility to our youth is, itself, a call to action.

While many have called the Pew Report an eye-opener, it is not a wholly critical eye that we should be opening. One of the best traits that we can acquire is a positive outlook, for it allows us to see the good possibilities that life can offer. Another is the ability to envision the consequences of our actions, for it can motivate us to continue pushing forward. In this landmark issue, Jewish leaders have come together and have shown us a possible world and a path on which to proceed. They are leaders whom I would readily follow for they embody another of Hillel's perceptive maxims, "Do not separate yourself from the community. Do not believe in yourself [alone] until the day you die. Do not judge your fellow until you have stood in his place."

The Pew Survey Reanalyzed: More Bad News, But a Glimmer of Hope

Jack Wertheimer, Steven M. Cohen

➤ **Dr. Jack Wertheimer** is the Joseph and Martha Mendelson Professor of American Jewish History at The Jewish Theological Seminary.

➤ **Dr. Steven M. Cohen** is Research Professor of Jewish Social Policy at HUC-JIR, and Director of the Berman Jewish Policy Archive at NYU Wagner.

Last year's survey of American Jews brought dire news—rising intermarriage, falling birthrates, dwindling congregations. Our reanalysis confirms the message, and complicates it.

A year has now elapsed since the Pew Research Center released its "Portrait of Jewish Americans," based on the first national survey of its kind in over a decade. Conducted by a leading "fact tank," as Pew describes itself, and based on the responses of over 5,000 individuals identifying themselves as Jews or claiming some other connection, real or imagined, with Jewishness, the report sparked numerous articles summarizing its key findings and commenting on their significance. It also prompted intense discussions within Jewish institutions, from synagogues to Jewish federations and communal agencies.

But as the weeks and months passed, and as few if any new policies emerged to address the Pew findings,

the conversation petered out. Today, the study's major conclusions—on the relentless growth in rates of intermarriage, on the falling birthrates and attenuating affiliations of non-Orthodox Jews, and much more of a distressing nature—seem to have receded far into the background of American Jewish consciousness.

This muted reaction stands in marked contrast to the communal response to the National Jewish Population Study conducted in 1990. In the face of that earlier survey's disclosure of marked weaknesses in Jewish life, local and national organizations formed task forces to chart new policy directions, including new initiatives in Jewish education of which the founding of Birthright Israel became the best known and among the most positively consequential. Nothing comparable has been put in place since the appearance of the Pew report; nor is there evidence of anything significant on the horizon.

Why the tepid response? For one

The Pew Survey Reanalyzed: More Bad News, But a Glimmer of Hope

thing, conventional wisdom in many quarters has it that the report actually offered little news; at worst, long-standing patterns have simply continued to unfold. Some have justified their indifference by noting the report's limitations: it offers only a snapshot in time, its questions were not designed either to produce or to assess policy outcomes, its categorization of Jews in largely religious terms was questionable, and so forth. A few optimists, seizing on the high number of Americans now claiming to be Jewish in some sense or other, even hailed the report's demographic statistics as cheering.

Before these essentially dismissive attitudes take permanent hold, a fresh look at the Pew findings is in order. In what follows, we base ourselves primarily on a reanalysis of data gathered by the Pew survey but that did not make their way into its published findings. Our focus is not on the socio-economic mobility, general educational attainments, or other measures of Jewish achievement in America. Rather, we focus on how Jews relate to Judaism, Jewish institutions and causes, and what if anything they are doing to perpetuate Jewish life in the United States. The exercise should tell us a good deal about the American Jewish condition—a condition that is dire enough to warrant the serious attention of anyone concerned about the Jewish

future.

1. The Tales American Jews Tell Themselves

Contrary to claims that the Pew report merely substantiates what we have long known, it actually offers powerful evidence to refute some of the most cherished myths of American Jewish life.

Take, for example, the pride Jews take in the strength and exemplary qualities of their family life. In theory, marriage and procreation are high ideals of Judaism, and much has been said and written about the ways in which the family has historically anchored Jews at times of joy and celebration, served as a haven of comfort during times of trouble, and guaranteed the continuity of the Jewish people. Even in our own time, this idea of Jewish family life as an impregnable fortress has remained all but sacrosanct.

In theory, marriage and procreation are high ideals of Judaism. But the fact is that fewer and fewer American Jews are actually getting married and forming families in the first place.

But how can any such idea withstand the plain fact that declining proportions of American Jews are actually getting married and forming families in the first place? At the time of the Pew survey, fewer than a third of non-Orthodox Jewish males and barely two-fifths of Jewish women

The Pew Survey Reanalyzed: More Bad News, But a Glimmer of Hope

between the ages of twenty-five and thirty-nine were married. (The smaller, Orthodox population is excluded from our calculations because its overall family patterns are so different.) For those between forty and fifty-four, the marriage rate climbs, but does not exceed 68 percent for men or 58 percent for women. While a small proportion of the unmarried are living with partners, close to a fifth of non-Orthodox American Jews never "couple off" during the conventional child-bearing years.

Perhaps even more startling, about the same proportion of Jews just past the prime childbearing years have never become parents. In other words, not only are today's younger generations delaying family formation, but increasing proportions are eschewing it altogether. Reasons can be adduced for these patterns (which are not dissimilar to those of secular, urban, and college-educated non-Jews as well), but the point remains: the choices made by a good many Jews hardly support the notion that Jews are paragons of family-mindedness.

A related fable American Jews tell about themselves is how child-oriented they are. Not only are they justly reputed to invest themselves significantly in their children's education and social advancement at every stage, from pre-school to college and beyond, but this same sharp focus on the child also too often characterizes their relation to Judaism and Jewish institutions. Not surprisingly, Hanukkah candle-lighting and Passover seders, two highly child-centered practices, are the religious rituals most widely observed by American Jews. On the average, weekly Sabbath, it is not the regular service for adults, but a bar- or bat-mitzvah celebration that draws family and friends to the synagogue.

And yet, for all their child-centeredness, many Jews seem either unable to find partners with whom to have children or are not all that interested in having children in the first place. Overall, an analysis of the Pew data indicates a fertility level of about 1.7 children for non-Orthodox Jews, well below the replacement level of 2.1 children. The shrinkage is already visible, having resulted in a drop of nearly one-third in the cohort of non-Orthodox Jews under the age of seventeen as compared with the cohort between the ages of forty and fifty-seven. (Again by contrast, the smaller population of Orthodox Jews, at 4.1 children per couple, has been growing both in absolute and relative terms.)

Presumably, it would be of great communal interest to learn whether anything can be done to reverse the self-defeating fertility rates within so much of the American Jewish populace. But even in the absence of explanations or recommendations, it

The Pew Survey Reanalyzed: More Bad News, But a Glimmer of Hope

ought to be clear that what once was the strong suit of the American Jewish community—its family values and its child-centeredness—is now, when it comes to perpetuating that community, one of its greatest weaknesses.

Or take intermarriage, another issue that Pew illuminates more starkly than any previous study. Ever since findings released in 1990 showed dramatically increasing rates of exogamy, there has been much discussion of this issue in communal circles. Traditionalists have been appalled both on religious grounds—Judaism has long prohibited intermarriage—and on pragmatic grounds: it is exceedingly difficult to raise children committed to Jewish life in families with two separate religions. Decades ago, Milton Himmelfarb made the point succinctly when he was asked what the grandchild of an intermarried Jew should be called. "A Christian," he answered.

But large sectors of the Jewish community have rejected this conclusion as unnecessarily defeatist or wrong. Speaking after the release of the Pew report, Rabbi Rick Jacobs, president of the Union for Reform Judaism, proclaimed: "being 'against' intermarriage is like being 'against' gravity." Several organizations now work to persuade the wider Jewish public that what prevents more intermarried families from joining synagogues and participating in Jewish life is only the Jews' own failure to be sufficiently "welcoming."

The Pew findings unequivocally support Himmelfarb's more hardheaded conclusion. Among those findings: as many as 2,100,000 Americans of some Jewish parentage—overwhelmingly, the offspring of intermarried parents—do not identify themselves as Jews. Our analysis of Pew and other national and local surveys also shows that intermarried families are considerably less likely to join synagogues, contribute to Jewish charities, identify strongly with Israel, observe Jewish religious rituals, or befriend other Jews. Exceptions aside, the large majority of intermarried families are loosely, ambivalently, or not at all connected to Jewish life.

What we know about the adult children of intermarried parents is even less heartening. It is true that among all such adults between the ages of eighteen and twenty-nine, as many as 59 percent identify as Jews. For Ted Sasson of Brandeis University, these are grounds for cautious optimism. But until these eighteen-to-twenty-nine-year-olds themselves marry, we can only speculate about their later relation to Jewish life—and on this score, there is little cause for optimism. When children of intermarriage do choose a spouse, reports Pew, 83 percent follow their parents' model and marry non-Jews. To project even farther

The Pew Survey Reanalyzed: More Bad News, But a Glimmer of Hope

into the future, a mere 8 percent of grandchildren of the intermarried are likely to marry Jews.

And how could matters be otherwise, given what intermarried families told Pew about how they raise their children? Among the non-Orthodox population between ages twenty-five and fifty-four, 36 percent of mixed-marrieds are not raising children as Jewish at all, and 44 percent say their children are being raised partly as Jews or as Jewish but with no Jewish religion. That leaves only 20 percent claiming to raise their children exclusively in the Jewish religion. (For comparison's sake, the equivalent figure for parents in in-married homes is 93 percent.).

In addition to its data on aspects of family life, the Pew report also sheds light on the participation of America's Jews in group or communal activities. In the 1960s, Fortune magazine rhapsodized in particular over the "the miracle of Jewish giving." For their part, Jews have historically taken pride not only in their well-documented altruism but in their shared sense of connection with and responsibility for their fellow Jews.

No longer. Fewer than one-third of Pew's national sample have joined a synagogue or regard belonging to a Jewish community as an essential part of Jewish identity. As for charitable giving to Jewish causes, it is eschewed by over 40 percent of American Jews. Although considerably higher percentages donate to non-sectarian causes, supporting Jewish philanthropy is no longer a given.

Social interactions among American Jews are also on the wane. Fewer than one in three claim mostly Jewish friends, and over one-fifth report none. The most weakly connected of all are in the Sunbelt and West Coast regions that are now attracting Jewish migrants; there, even larger numbers shun connections with other Jews, affiliation with Jewish institutions, or giving to Jewish causes.

This failure of group connectedness is having serious consequences for organized Jewish life. It is no secret that most federations of Jewish philanthropy and other communal institutions are being forced to rely on shrinking numbers of supporters, or that the federation system attracts considerably fewer than half the number of gifts it received just a few decades ago. Correlatively, the membership rolls of Jewish organizations have been greatly reduced, and the programs offered by Jewish institutions draw significantly fewer takers.

To put all of this in generational terms: wherever we look, we find age-related declines in the number of non-Orthodox Jews who are active in Jewish life. Comparing thirty-to-forty-nine-year-olds with those twenty years older, we see about half as many who are

The Pew Survey Reanalyzed: More Bad News, But a Glimmer of Hope

members of synagogues or of Jewish organizations, or who donate to any Jewish cause. Roughly similar declines affect the numbers feeling very attached to Israel, or saying that being Jewish is very important to them, or having close friends who are mostly Jewish.

No other major Western Jewish community displays such low levels of Jewish literacy, or sends such a small proportion of its people on trips to Israel.

What does this mean? Not only are there, to begin with, far fewer non-Orthodox Jews in the younger age cohort (about 1.2 million vs. 1.8 million), but the proportion of those younger Jews who are active or committed is itself smaller as well; on every measure of Jewish identity, those between thirty and forty-nine trail substantially behind those between fifty and sixty-nine. This, in turn, leaves those who are still interested and active in Jewish life much less likely to find family members, friends, colleagues, or community members who are similarly involved. The preponderance of so many inactive non-Orthodox Jews in their prime childbearing years cannot but foreshadow further declines in the next generation.

Altogether, as Jewish institutions speak for fewer and fewer constituents, Jewish group life becomes more attenuated, episodic, and impoverished. In this respect as in the others we have described, organized American Jewry lags behind its counterparts in Canada, England, France, Australia, and South Africa. No other major Western Jewish community displays such low levels of Jewish literacy, enrolls so small a proportion of its children in Jewish day schools, or sends such a small proportion of its people on trips to Israel. If Pew tells us anything, it is this: judged by their ability to retain the allegiance of their young, foster a commitment to the group life of Jews at home and abroad, or even meet the elementary needs of survival, American Jews, whatever stories they continue to tell about themselves, no longer constitute a great community.

2. The Exceptions, and What They Tell Us

If the overall picture is of a community weakened and unhealthy, a closer examination yields instructive examples of subgroups that are either positively thriving or doing a relatively good job of supporting communal life and transmitting a strong sense of Jewish connection to the next generation. There is much to be learned from these examples.

First, on the broadest level, Jews who identify themselves with the Jewish religion are far more engaged with all aspects of Jewish life than are Jews lacking such an identification. By "all aspects," we mean not only such obvious

The Pew Survey Reanalyzed: More Bad News, But a Glimmer of Hope

things as synagogue attendance and ritual observance but also connection to Israel, engagement in non-religious Jewish organizations, likelihood of giving to Jewish causes, and forging close friendships with other Jews.

And that is on the broadest level. Even more striking is that the specific religious denomination in which Jews are raised—Orthodox, Conservative, Reform, or otherwise—carries major implications for the choices they make as adults. Overall, a "denominational gradient" holds true: those raised Orthodox tend to be the most engaged, followed by those raised Conservative, followed by those raised Reform, followed by those raised with no denomination.

Our analysis of the Pew data challenges two commonly held beliefs about the state of denominationalism in Jewish life today. For one thing, the widely touted phenomenon of post- or non-denominationalism—allegedly, the leading edge of a new American Judaism—requires rethinking: on every measure, Jews by religion who were raised in no denomination evince lower levels of Jewish connection than do Jews raised in some denomination.

Jews under the age of fifty who have been raised Conservative exhibit far higher rates of connection than do their Reform counterparts.

For another—and very intriguing—thing, the Pew findings also refute the notion that a convergence is taking place that will erase the differences between, for example, Conservative and Reform Judaism. As we saw above, if we take non-Orthodox Jews as a whole, there has been a striking decline in Jewish activity or commitment among those under the age of fifty. But when we compare specific denominations of the non-Orthodox, we find striking differences in levels of Jewish engagement. In fact, those differences are more pronounced among younger Jews than among their elders.

This pattern is especially evident with regard to the sense of belonging to and of responsibility for the Jewish people; on this measure, Jews under the age of fifty who have been raised Conservative exhibit far higher rates of connection than do their Reform counterparts. Similarly large gaps open between those raised Conservative and those raised Reform when it comes to levels of attachment to Israel, participation in religious life, joining Jewish organizations, and having mostly Jewish friends. The same can be said about rates of intermarriage and about the family decisions made by intermarried parents. Indeed, the variance in intermarriage rates alone is so stark—in the period 2000-2013, 39 percent of Conservative-raised Jews intermarried versus 82 percent of those raised Reform—as to suggest that we are faced with two different sets of

The Pew Survey Reanalyzed: More Bad News, But a Glimmer of Hope

attitudes and practices.

These findings must be tempered by the sobering reality that both the Conservative- and the Reform-affiliated populations have been shrinking. The two major movements outside of Orthodoxy are losing market share: only 11 percent of American Jewish adults are members of Conservative synagogues, and only 14 percent are members of Reform temples. Nevertheless, it is blindingly clear that so-called liberal Jews are not all the same. Instead, Jews select and remain in a particular denomination because its ethos conforms to their own self-understanding and style of Jewish living. If anything, that tendency has grown over time.

A second critical axis of differentiation among Jews concerns education. Here the gradient of engagement extends downward from the high of those who have attended day schools for nine or more years, to those with seven years of supplementary schooling plus a Jewish summer-camp experience, to those with progressively fewer years of supplementary schooling, and finally to those who have received no Jewish education and who are correspondingly the least likely to be engaged in Jewish life. (In fact, among non-Orthodox Jews between the ages of eighteen and twenty-nine, nearly half have received either no Jewish education or just six years or less of supplementary

schooling. These minimal exposures speak to family priorities.)

The same pattern applies regarding marriage and other indices. If, in the aggregate, more Jewish education means more Jewish engagement, more Jewish education also means higher levels of in-marriage. Similarly, those with more intensive Jewish educational experiences are most likely to be raising their children in the Jewish religion, to feel a sense of responsibility for other Jews, and to participate in religious and synagogue life. In line with these data are findings on the beneficial impact of Jewish summer camps, especially those that combine camping with a strong educational mission, thereby offering an organic experience of Jewish life that reinforces and complements formal Jewish education of any kind.

In brief, the most sustained and immersive forms of Jewish education are associated with the best later outcomes. To imagine otherwise is illusory.

Third: endogamy, all by itself, matters. In the aggregate, individuals who have been raised by two Jewish parents make very different choices from those made by children of intermarried parents. We have already seen the marked tendency of the latter to marry non-Jews in their turn, and the relative unlikelihood of their raising their own children exclusively in the Jewish religion. Similar disparities can be shown on

The Pew Survey Reanalyzed: More Bad News, But a Glimmer of Hope

measures of religious participation and connection to the Jewish people, where adults raised by intermarried parents are, at most, only half as likely to be involved in the community as those raised by two Jewish parents; the gaps are even wider when it comes to joining synagogues, friendship with other Jews, and donating to Jewish charities.

The patterns traced by the Pew data, then, reinforce what common sense would tell us: Jewish identification and engagement are strengthened when young people are raised by two Jewish parents, exposed to many intensive Jewish educational experiences, and raised in homes tending toward traditional Judaism. In the aggregate, strong Jewish backgrounds make for later adult involvement.

Employing this general rule of thumb, can one proceed to construct communal policies that might pull American Jewish life back from the brink?

3. Rebuilding for a Better Future

A crucial first step is to acknowledge the seriousness of the situation. Whatever may be the number of Americans claiming some measure of Jewish identification, the proportion among them who, though of Jewish parentage, no longer identify themselves as Jews has never been higher. Not only that, but among identified Jews who are non-Orthodox, the levels

of disengagement from Jewish life— diminished social connections, shallow practice, attenuated involvements—are unprecedentedly high. If current trends continue, the identified American Jewish populace will consist increasingly of burgeoning communities of ultra-Orthodox (haredi) Jews and unengaged or "partial" Jews.

American Jews now stand on the precipice of a demographic cliff, and the choice before them is simple: either fall off, or turn around. Alas, much of organized Jewish life—which is to say, much of American Jewish leadership— shows no sense of urgency but proceeds as if a few small tweaks will miraculously reverse the destructive patterns eroding secular and non-Orthodox Jewish life. Seeing their roles as cheerleaders, reasoning that donors and volunteers can be recruited only if guaranteed of success, too many leaders cannot bring themselves to admit that American Jewry is in the midst of a deep-seated crisis. They therefore ignore not only the Pew data but, even more damagingly, a raft of other studies in recent decades that, for anyone truly interested in rebuilding American Jewish life, point to a number of ways out of the crisis.

All such studies make evident that the most effective initiatives share three critical features. (1) They create social networks that enhance interactions among Jews centering on matters

The Pew Survey Reanalyzed: More Bad News, But a Glimmer of Hope

of Jewish interest. (2) They target individuals in the same stages of life, enabling them to heighten their involvement in Jewish life along with their peers. And (3) they communicate Jewish content by exposing learners to sacred texts and the cultural heritage of the Jewish people.

With those three criteria in mind, let's turn to the most endangered but also the likeliest candidates for re-engagement, namely, those in the middle: Conservative and Reform Jews who are either in-married or intermarried but still committed to some form of Jewish life. And the most obvious place to begin is with their school-age children, who are still forming their identities. The Pew data underline the significance of both the time and the intensity devoted to early Jewish education. These are the immersion years, in which bedrock Jewish literacy is most easily acquired and the Hebrew language is most quickly assimilated. This makes it all the more tragic that day schools at every level have become largely the preserve of Orthodox Jews, with only small percentages of others choosing an immersive Jewish education for their children.

The challenge, therefore, is to persuade more Jewish parents to enroll their children in strong programs of Jewish education—and to support what those programs are teaching.

A properly organized Jewish effort would aim to increase the numbers of such parents and students by investing more philanthropic dollars in order to reduce tuition costs and by fighting for—rather than against—tax credits to offset those costs and stimulate greater philanthropic giving. (In this connection, it has been short-sighted in the extreme for philanthropies to stand idly by as Conservative institutions, especially Solomon Schechter day schools, have faltered; their decline or disappearance has impoverished the wider Jewish community.) Any such concerted effort should also seek to dispel the misconception that these schools cordon children off from participation in American society. The truth is that, in addition to offering a strong Jewish return on investment, most offer a first-rate general education and send their graduates on to elite colleges.

As young Jews enter their teen years, other forms of informal enrichment exist and need to be supported: residential summer camps offering serious Jewish content, Israel trips for sixteen- and seventeen-year-olds, youth groups. They also provide forms of intensive Jewish engagement for the many young people whose parents are unable, or unwilling, to send them to day schools. These programs work synergistically with each other and also with formal schooling during the

The Pew Survey Reanalyzed: More Bad News, But a Glimmer of Hope

critical high-school years. Rather than letting its teens fend for themselves after bar and bat mitzvah, a serious Jewish community would seek to embrace and excite them.

What about the college years? Several studies have shown that organized campus activities generally produce positive outcomes. The energetic growth of Chabad, some haredi groups, and a recent push by the Modern Orthodox movement have expanded opportunities for extracurricular Jewish learning and socializing on campus. But the messages conveyed by these programs do not always appeal to non-Orthodox Jews. Meanwhile, non-Orthodox personnel and models of engagement are rarely present on campuses, where they are greatly needed. Here, then, is another opportunity waiting to be seized.

As for the post-college years, we noted early on how the large majority of non-Orthodox Jews remain single and, if they marry, defer childbearing. Most connect to Jewish life episodically if at all, perhaps attending an occasional social or cultural event or joining their parents on a holiday. At this key period of life, when major decisions are being made, why has the Jewish community neglected to provide them with a rich menu of opportunities to remain involved?

Finally, for those who intermarry, why is there no concerted effort to invite Gentile partners and spouses to convert to Judaism? The differences between intermarried and so-called "conversionary" families are significant, with the latter much likelier to conduct themselves as do families in which both partners have been born Jewish. Conversion-oriented courses and institutes lead to more families that are exclusively committed to Jewish life, with all the attendant positive results—and here is yet another area of wise investment on the part of a community seeking to retain its members and ensure its future.

Beyond all of the initiatives outlined above lies the issue of quality: quality of life, and quality of standards. Jewish communities owe it to their members, especially the well-educated among them, to connect the two. The leaders of these communities need to explain to their members that just as a minimal Jewish education does a disservice to Jewish children, stunting their growth, a continuing immersion in Jewish life and Jewish learning invigorates the mind, nourishes the soul, and inspires the dedication of individuals and communities alike. They need to tell them that just as showing up sporadically at a Jewish event does nothing for a generation patently hungry for connection, more opportunities for Jews at every age level to come together with their peers for purposes of Jewish enrichment

The Pew Survey Reanalyzed: More Bad News, But a Glimmer of Hope

hold out the promise of making a transformative difference in their own lives and, through them, the life of their people. They need to tell them that just as intermarriage most often leads to disengagement from Jewish life, the advantages of in-marriage are positively salutary in their effect on Jewish family life and beyond, empowering all to claim their rightful role in the stream of the generations and instilling a healthy pride in a tradition transcending time and place.

At hand within the non-Orthodox sectors of the community—the Jewish middle—are reserves of human material that have gone unappreciated and shamefully underfunded.

Once engaged in content-rich Jewish learning, moreover, Jews of all ages can come to know and to possess a sense of transcendent purpose at once life-giving and defiantly at variance with today's faddish and often deadening emphasis on self-centered experience. Encountering the accumulated wisdom of a civilization with its own highly developed, deeply principled, and time-tested views on the largest existential and ethical issues faced by human beings, they can come to know and to recapture for themselves the bedrock courage and conviction that have differentiated and sustained both Judaism and the Jews through the ages. Absorbing the facts about contemporary Israel, its stunning achievements in nation-building in the face of a century of hostile threats, they will free themselves of reductionist narratives and take just pride in the epic project of the Jewish people unfolding before their eyes. Replacing atrophied Jewish reflexes with a muscular understanding of what it means to be part of a global and eternal people, they will come to know and to reclaim the truly universal blessing that flows from caring for and seeing to the perpetuation of one's own.

Such, at least, is our own conviction, and our stubborn hope.

Of course, for any of these initiatives to succeed, it will be necessary to reverse the self-defeating rationalizations that have taken hold in so many Jewish circles of Jewish leadership. A combination of ill-founded optimism, denial, and hopelessness has nurtured the belief that current patterns of Jewish life are acceptable and/or immutable. That belief is false: at hand within the non-Orthodox sectors of the community— what we have described as the Jewish middle—are reserves of human material that have gone unappreciated and shamefully underfunded. Rather than succumb to defeatist counsel, a new idealism is in order, grounded in hard-headed understanding of the parlous condition of American Jewry and the determination to redress it.

In the past, American Jews have mobilized to extend help to their

The Pew Survey Reanalyzed: More Bad News, But a Glimmer of Hope

coreligionists facing grave challenges abroad—Israelis in their battles against hostile neighbors, Russian Jews desperate to flee Soviet oppression, beleaguered Jews all over the world in need of rescue and succor. Can they now muster the will and resources to revitalize their own community? The task is immense; the hour is very late. But it is still possible to influence for the good, the size, the character, the commitment, and the spirit of American Jewry.

This article has been printed with the kind permission of Mosaic magazine. The original can be viewed on the magazine's website, at http://mosaicmagazine. com/essay/2014/11/the-pew-survey-reanalyzed/.

The Heart of the Matter

Sharon Brous

➤ *Rabbi Sharon Brous is the founding rabbi of IKAR, a community dedicated to reanimating Jewish life, standing at the intersection of soulful, inventive religious practice and a deep commitment to social justice.*

Years ago, at a conference, I got into an intense conversation about miracles with a young Jew from LA. He was smart, sensitive, and spiritually hungry. So, like a good rabbi, I suggested he come to Shabbat services sometime, and he laughed out loud. "If I want intellectual stimulation," he said, "I go to a TED conference. Spiritual enlightenment, I have a shaman. Community? Burning Man. I don't need shul."

The past several years have revealed, both empirically and statistically, that my friend is not anomalous—the established Jewish community has failed to capture the imagination of young Jews. Perhaps the most salient statistic emerging from last year's Pew Study on the American Jewish community (aside from the 4% of Orthodox Jews with Christmas trees in their homes) was the 22% who consider themselves Jews of no religion. These are people who were raised as Jews and identify as Jews, but when asked their religion—Jewish, Christian, Muslim, other, or none—they choose "none."

It's not just that they're not synagogue members (if that were the question, the statistics would be significantly higher—estimates are that closer to 75% of American Jews are unaffiliated with a synagogue), it's that they claim to be disconnected from Judaism as a religion. This is a stunning finding. While, for centuries, there have been thriving Jewish communities that were de-coupled from Jewish faith assumptions and ritual observance, there is now a widespread population of Jews—nearly one quarter—disavowing connection to the Jewish religion altogether.

I have spent the past decade speaking with thousands of those who would have identified as "Jews of no religion" had they answered the phone when the Pew researchers called. And while I wouldn't claim that the findings are particularly good news, I do believe that there is a real silver lining, revealed once we ask the "nones" what it is that really repels and compels them. Here's what I have learned, working

➤ The Heart of the Matter

with and living among this population of predominantly young, decidedly unaffiliated, religiously disconnected Jews:

I have not yet heard one who rejects the idea of powering down once a week in order to step out of the world as it is and imagine the world as it could be. Not one marginalized or ambivalent Jew I've spoken with has resisted the wisdom of changing her rhythm in order to reconnect with her most audacious dreams, realign with her priorities, and spend time with the people she loves most. In other words, I have yet to meet an unaffiliated, disconnected Jew who fundamentally rejects the idea of Shabbat.

I have shared with hundreds of "Jews of no religion" the spiritual practice of waking up each morning with words of gratitude on our lips. Not one has rejected the idea, nor has anyone objected to the idea of offering words of forgiveness just before bed. Many have even hungrily embraced the words of modeh ani (I am grateful) and the language of kriyat sh'ma al ha-mita (bedtime sh'ma).

I daven (pray) every Shabbat with many so-called Jews of no religion. What I have seen is real prayer, even despite all the ambivalence, cynicism, and doubt. I have seen many come week after week, holding in their hands a book written in a language they can't read and filled with theological images they find disturbing, and, nevertheless, singing with all their hearts, sometimes crying, sometimes even dancing.

Even those who wish we served bacon maple donuts at Kiddush do not reject the idea that when we eat mindfully, we can bring holiness into an otherwise mundane act.

Even non-religious Jews know and understand that ritual can move them to tears, or that it can fill their hearts with wonder, appreciation, and a deep sense of connection. Some even feel, in ritual, the presence of God.

While many shun identification with organized religion, I have yet to encounter one who rejects the idea of community, of showing up for one another in times of celebration and grief, of dancing with one other in moments of joy, of sitting in silence in moments of pain, of saying amen when someone else needs to say Yitgadal v'yitkadash sh'mei rabbah (May His great Name grow exalted and sanctified, Mourner's Prayer).

I have not yet encountered opposition to the contention that religious environments ought not only nurture the soul, but also awaken in us a sense of connectedness to and responsibility for one another.

I have yet to meet a Jew, no matter how disaffected, disinterested, or disgusted, who rejects the idea that the most routine moments in our lives, from going to the bathroom to eating a snack

➤ The Heart of the Matter

to drinking a caramel Frappuccino, can be elevated if we take a moment to express gratitude.

I have yet to meet a secular, disconnected Jew who couldn't find in Biblical and Talmudic narratives an echo of his own struggles and moral quandaries, insights into living a rich and meaningful life.

But if they are not rejecting the core elements of Jewish religious life— Shabbat, kashrut, community, prayer, ritual, gratitude, forgiveness, holiness, God—what, then, are a quarter to a third of American Jews opposing when they disavow a connection to the Jewish religion?

The Heart of the Matter

David Steindl-Rast, a Benedictine monk, explains better than anyone I know what is broken at the heart of organized religion. Religion, he says, is like an erupting volcano: the lava flowing down the sides of the mountain – fiery, powerful, dangerous, "gushing forth red hot from the depths of mystical consciousness." But the stream of lava quickly cools off. A couple hundred years pass, and what was once alive is now dead rock, devoid of all traces of life. "Doctrine becomes doctrinaire. Morals become moralistic. Ritual becomes ritualistic… All are layers of ash deposits and volcanic rock that separate us from the fiery magma deep down below" (See *The Mystical*

Core of Organized Religion and *Lunch With Bokara*).

The religious system and its institutions began as containers designed to hold the sacred experience, preserve its power, and extend its reverberations. But these containers, because one can touch them and mold them and compulsively ruminate over them, begin to obscure the very core they were designed to preserve. When that happens, rather than give people access to profound spiritual and religious inspiration, the containers themselves become an obstacle to inspiration.

And this seems to be precisely what is happening in American religious life today, thus the unprecedented disaffection, defection and overriding sense of disinterest among American Jews, especially young ones. The silver lining is that they are not rejecting Judaism at all. They don't reject Jewish identity, community, or rituals. They don't reject Jewish ideas. It's not even God that they reject.

They reject a 20th-century iteration of Jewish religious life that just feels too many layers away from the sacred fire. It feels devoid of life, passion, spiritual challenge. Judaism in America too often seems to be more concerned with the container–the formalities, rules, and rites–than the fire—the soul and spirit, the mystical core. The heart of the matter. Jews often appear to be more concerned with what you wear

➤ The Heart of the Matter

than where you are. Too often it feels like institutional perpetuation for its own sake.

The Challenge

The challenge then becomes: How can we honor a hunger for connection, for spiritual depth and meaning, and for ritual and for community, but free ourselves of the dead rock and ash deposit of 20th-century institutional religious life?

Some answers may be found in a notable countertrend in the American Jewish community: a rebooting of established institutions and the creation of newly empowered, inspired communities around the country. None of these approaches is revolutionary, but taken together, they may help pave the way for deeper and more meaningful engagement. I do not want to suggest that organizational change is easy, but I have come to understand that we are often working at cross-purposes with ourselves, undermining our long-term goals (helping Jews find relevance and meaning in the Jewish tradition) by holding fast to temporal mechanisms (elements of institutional culture that no longer resonate). And that we need to and can change.

Discomfort is a Spiritual Objective

The first principle of vibrant, vital organizations may be counter-instinctual: Discomfort is essential to growth. Abraham Joshua Heschel argues in *Man's Quest for God*: "Assembled in the synagogue everything is there--the body, the benches, the books. But one thing is absent: soul. It is as if we all suffered from spiritual absenteeism... In our synagogues, people who are otherwise sensitive, vibrant, arresting, sit there aloof, listless, lazy."

Our prayer services have become so rehearsed, so perfunctory, that they rarely pierce the surface, let alone penetrate the heart. In Heschel's words, we read the prayer book as if reading paragraphs in Roget's Thesaurus. "Of course," he writes, "they are offered plenty of responsive reading, but there is little responsiveness to what they read. No one knows how to shed a tear. No one is ready to invest a sigh. Is there no tear in their souls?"

How do we create, once again, the space for tears in our services? For movement, for spontaneity and vulnerability?

One Friday afternoon last year, I realized that I was bored with our Kabbalat Shabbat services. I checked in with my colleagues, who admitted that they felt similarly uninspired by what had become our routine. We quickly determined that we'd experiment with moving the service into a room one third the size. We removed all the chairs and posted a couple of signs that read: Discomfort is Better than Boredom. An hour later, a few hundred

➤ The Heart of the Matter

people arrived for services. They were confused, agitated, and uncomfortable. Most refused even to step into the room. The night was a dismal failure. So we did it again. This time everyone came in, but they all stood in straight rows, stiff as soldiers. By the third try, people moved. They danced and sang. Many cried. It was a breakthrough moment for our community. Many people subsequently told me they had never davened until that service—it was the first time they felt free enough to express what was in their hearts.

We had become so habituated to our limitations--environment, formal rules of a prayer service ("please rise/ please be seated")—that we had forsaken our own spiritual freedom.

Discomfort wakes us up. It takes the community—and the leadership—by surprise. If we are willing to fail publicly, to experiment when there is no reasonable assurance that we'll succeed, we build spiritually vital communities. Sometimes the best moments of our services come when we start on the wrong page or in the wrong key, laugh and adjust or stop in the middle of a service that's not working and ask that everyone stand up and move around, come join us in the middle of the room, or talk about what's amiss and start over. We try every Shabbat to take some risk, dive into discomfort, and honor the learning that comes from failure.

Don't Sacrifice Depth for Inclusion

Someone noted in IKAR's early days that our organizing principle was lower the bar for entry, raise the bar for engagement. In other words, make sure every person feels seen and welcomed when she enters the room, but do not mistake access with ease. Too often our communities err in diluting powerful texts, claims, rituals, and ideas from our tradition so as not to leave anyone feeling alienated. Our theory, instead, was that if we speak honestly about the mysterious power of our rituals, if we invite people to challenge themselves with our rituals and traditions, extraordinary and unpredictable outcomes might emerge. At High Holy Days now we have 1,500 Jews–cynical, disaffected, and atheistic—prostrating fully to the ground, weeping, and then rising up with their hands to the heavens, holding the paradox of powerlessness and power.

I have found that when we tell people something is asked of them, they are inspired to learn more— and when we speak in a language of experimentation, there's nothing people won't try. As long as we acknowledge the complexity and foreignness of many of our rituals, people open up. For two years, our adult learning program, called Get Unstuck, was rooted in the assumption that a small practice might hold the power to change a person's life. Each month we challenged the community

➤ The Heart of the Matter

to experiment with very specific Jewish spiritual or ritual practices, introducing various points of access to the tradition. We were impressed and moved by people's hunger to try to find meaning in very old practices and their willingness to be challenged to experiment with something completely new.

Culture Matters. Message Matters.

Before we founded IKAR, I spent a couple of years working as a rabbi-in-residence at a large, thriving Jewish community high school. One week, an expert on organizational culture and psychology arrived to conduct an evaluation of our school. The school was dedicated to unearthing core Jewish teachings of hesed and tzedakah, love and justice, and integrating all aspects of school life with those values, from our dress code to our sophisticated interdisciplinary curriculum. I prepared for the meeting alongside my senior colleagues in the administration. We were confident that the expert would note how seamlessly daily life on campus was infused with our core message. When he arrived, we walked him around campus, proudly demonstrating how we used open space to create collaborative work environments, used natural light to reflect the permeability of Jewish life—we were in constant, dynamic conversation with the world around

us. He silently observed, taking note of every detail, from the entry gate to the bathroom stalls. Finally, he sat us down and offered his assessment: "I know you think this school is about Torah, avodah (worship), and g'milut hadsadim (deeds of loving kindness)," he said. "But I hear three other messages: 1) Everyone wants to kill the Jews [the first thing you see as you approach campus is a high security fence and guards]; 2) We want your money [the one giant banner on the front of the entry gate reads "Capital Campaign – Help Us Reach 100% Participation"; and 3) You're already late [a large clock is positioned prominently on the building exterior, looking out over a busy freeway]. You don't want to be communicating these messages," he said, "but you are—loud and clear. And let me tell you: Those are hard messages to counteract."

This began my education in organizational culture. A few years later I flew to Philadelphia to officiate at the wedding of an old friend. The wedding was scheduled to start just after Shabbat ended, so Saturday morning I got up early and went for a long walk, landing at a well-known synagogue just in time for services. Walking in, I was greeted by two large signs posted by the doors: NO CELL-PHONES and NO PAGERS. "Shabbat shalom to you too," I thought. Since then, I have strongly advocated periodic walks through our own buildings with fresh, critical eyes.

➤ The Heart of the Matter

What are the unintended messages we're sending that are repelling rather than attracting people, especially those who may be predisposed to dislike institutional religious environments?

Here's what we've posted on the walls outside the space where we gather:

Welcome to IKAR. Our tradition is to POWER DOWN on Shabbat, because sometimes we have to go off the grid to make room for something holy. We invite you to join us (you never know what might happen…).

(at the bottom of a long staircase on the way into the building:)

Welcome to IKAR—you're almost there! We promise to make it worth your while.

(at the check-in table at High Holy Days, where 2000 people clamor for the attention of four staff members at once:)

Shana tova. We're doing our best to get you inside for your spiritual recharge. Please remember that it's Yom Kippur out here in the lobby too—and be kind to our staff and one another.

(on the walls of our davening space:)

IN A WORLD…

of political turmoil
social alienation
technological hyperdrive
environmental devastation
personal upheaval
and really bad traffic –
let's try something a little different.
power down.

breathe.
be present.
be grateful.
change your rhythm. change the world.
shabbat shalom, and welcome to IKAR.

(and at the entrance to our standing-only Friday night service:)

Don't worry - you're in the right place. We're just doing things a bit differently tonight.

We've found that our spirits are more likely to move if our bodies aren't crammed into uncomfortable chairs. Or even worse, comfortable chairs. So come on in and get uncomfortable.

Sing. Even off-key. Even if you don't know Hebrew.

Stomp. Clap. Shake your moneymaker. Close your eyes.

Open your heart and your mouth.

Be grateful. Be great.

Shabbat shalom, and welcome to IKAR.

The way that we message who we are and what we're trying to accomplish shapes people's experience and opens them up to new possibilities. Culture is too important to be left up to chance.

Embrace the Contradictions

When I first applied for rabbinic positions after ordination, one search committee head said he thought I wouldn't be happy in his synagogue because I was an activist. Their

➤ The Heart of the Matter

community, he explained, cared about Talmud Torah, the study and teaching of Torah. "If what you care about is feeding the hungry," he said, "go to the synagogue down the street."

Here's the problem: Our tradition is multifaceted and our people are smart. We don't have to choose between personal meaning and world-on-fire Judaism. Why is it that the communities that stand at the forefront of social change issues— gun violence prevention, marriage equality, racial and economic justice, immigration reform—are generally not known for the power and depth of their prayer experiences? Why have we segregated out the parts of the Jewish heart, essentially making people choose between a Shabbes davening community or a community of fellow activists? We have to build more holistic and integrated models that honor both theology and practice, the community and the individual, the particular and the universal, keva (fixed and established practice) and kavannah (creative, imaginative, heartfelt expression). Our hearts are capacious and capable of holding complexities.

Substance Matters More than Space

There are about 3,700 synagogues in America, many housed in large, beautiful buildings. But many young Jews have a kind of institutional allergy. Like it or not, they simply will not walk through the doors of the synagogue, which means that the only way to connect with them is to leave the walls of the synagogue and seek people out in the environments in which they feel most comfortable—bars, living rooms, cafes, art studios. Over the past ten years, we've held house parties nearly every week in people's homes. We cap registration at the number of people who can fit comfortably in the hosts' living room and choose topics based on what's most interesting or compelling to the host at that time—everything from "Why Do My Friends and I Still Struggle with Body Image– We're Almost 30?" to "How Do I Talk to My Kids About God When I Don't Know If I Believe?" to questions about fertility struggles, finding one's purpose, being lonely. People are much more willing to engage if they don't have to first overcome the environmental obstacle, and much more likely to study traditional texts if they care about the topic. People's guards are down in their friends' homes, especially if there's wine and cheese. We hold regular "Get In The Know" events in bars, where people write their questions on large Post-it notes on the walls, the rabbis are given an open mic, and we talk for hours about the real issues touching real people. We've found that once we have established a relationship in a non-threatening environment, people are much more likely to come to

⟫ The Heart of the Matter

Shabbat services.

I don't know that my friend will ever choose shul over his shaman. But I do know that while the demographic freefall is irrefutable, it is not immutable. We are standing at the threshold of a new chapter in American Jewish life. If we listen carefully, we'll hear a distancing from the last century's container–but not the essence of Jewish life. We'll hear a hunger for an inclusive, compassionate, and connective Jewish experience, one that is courageous and challenging, imaginative and uninhibited. One that, as Rav Kook taught, strives to make the old new and the new holy. I hope that we'll honor that voice, help reclaim the sacred essence of our tradition, and redefine, as every generation must, what it really means to be a Jew in the world.

Envisioning a Jewish Future

Arthur Green

➤ **Rabbi Dr. Arthur Green** is the Irving Brudnick Professor of Jewish Philosophy and Religion and Rector of the Rabbinical School at Hebrew College in Newton MA. He can be reached at agreen@hebrewcollege.edu.

Let us begin by distinguishing between two questions. The posed "What will American Jewry look like in ten years?" includes various elements – deeper assimilation, higher intermarriage rates, increasing disillusionment with Israel, etc. – all of which seem quite inevitable, despite our greatest efforts to prevent them. "What might American Jewry look like in ten years?" is a question that invites vision, mine and that of the Hebrew College Rabbinical School (HCRS), which I founded in 2004. Our rabbinical school has just taken in the largest new student group in its history, which is also the largest incoming group of students in any single-site non-Orthodox rabbinical school in the country. We are a factor to be reckoned with in the shaping of future leadership for our shared community. We are, therefore, compelled to ask, how might Jewish life look different if a significant percentage of America's rabbis are trained at Hebrew College, or at other institutions shaped by our influence?

I have, in fact, had a fairly consistent view of American Jewish life, its spiritual ills and some ways of healing it, since founding Havurat Shalom in 1968, the beginning of what came to be known as the "Havurah movement," though regrettably never organized as such. The opportunity to work in several different institutional contexts over the years has sharpened my perspective, but the essential value-system has remained surprisingly constant across nearly half a century.

The synagogue remains the key institution of American Jewry. Despite the fact that Jews measure as the most secularized ethnic/religious group on the American scene, no secular institution, such as the JCC, has significantly displaced the synagogue as the center of Jewish life. There are two reasons for this, one external and the other internal. From the outside, we are living in the most religious of any advanced society the world has seen. Church affiliation is important to Americans. As we moved from the ethnically monolithic urban

➤ Envisioning a Jewish Future

neighborhoods out into white suburbia between 1950 and 1975, Jews needed to show our WASP neighbors that we, too, had a place of worship, one with which we proudly identified, even if we attended quite irregularly, as did many of them. Internally and more significantly, secularized Jews are not nearly quite so secular as statistics have portrayed them. If you define secularism by the pollsters' questions, "Do you believe in God?" or "Do you believe in a personal afterlife?" you will indeed see a very high degree of secularity. But if the question focuses on practice, particularly around the defining issue of the personal life cycle, as in, "Do you want a Bar/Bat Mitzvah for your child?" or "Do you want to be married/ buried/mourned as a Jew?" you will see evidence of a very high identification with Jewish religious praxis. True, on the regular year-cycle observances the statistics will be lower, but there, too, they have improved dramatically in recent decades, including among intermarried families. Witness Passover seders, Hanukkah candles, even the rebirth of such unpredictable "oddities" as Tu Bi-Shvat and Tikkun Leyl Shavu'ot.

What does all this mean for the future, and specifically for our approach? Let me provide you with two answers:

1. The synagogue functions primarily as a place of prayer. Prayer is not easy for non-Orthodox American Jews, most of whom are not sure if they believe in God, and almost all of whom do not think God answers prayer in the ordinary sense of that term. How, then, will we make the synagogue work? This is not a question that can be answered simplistically or in a singular way; a variety of approaches need to be tried. Creativity is the key; the old service, whether standard Conservative or Reform, no longer suffices. Such creativity must include new versions of the prayer book (including remarkable recent achievements within each of the liberal movements), new music, silence, movement, guided meditation, and lots more. The synagogue of the future has multiple worship experiences offered simultaneously, serving a variety of spiritual and emotional needs. These all depend upon greater cultivation of spiritual awareness as a key dimension of human life. Open discussion of such often taboo topics as God's love, mortality, doubt, and the quest for personal meaning are all necessary components. Above all, meaningful prayer experiences do not just happen; they require creative thought, insight, and planning.

2. No matter what rabbis and synagogues do, prayer will remain difficult for a large part of the Jewish population. That is simply a reality of the secular age in which we live. But that

➤ Envisioning a Jewish Future

is not true of Jewish learning. Today's Jews, virtually all of whom are college graduates, thirst for Jewish knowledge. The success of various higher-level adult study courses (Hebrew College's own Meah, Wexner, Melton, Limmud, etc.) attest to this. If Jewish texts and ideas are presented on a high level, with room for lots of interactive participation in the commentary and understanding processes, many Jews will be attracted to such learning. The synagogue needs to be converted into an interactive Bet Midrash, House of Study. Learning should become its best-known and most popular activity. The synagogue should be as full on Tuesday evening Bet Midrash night as it is for Shabbat services. HCRS's greatest success has been in imbuing our students with a sense of ahavat Torah, a genuine love of Jewish learning, and a sense that text study, especially in small groups or hevruta pairs, is the fast-beating heart of Jewish education. Our graduates are sent forth with a very clear message that the synagogue needs to become a House of Study. This should include groups engaged in studying Torah, TaNaKH, Mishnah, Talmud, Zohar, Hasidic sources, classical and modern Hebrew poetry, Jewish arts and fiction, and lots more. The future of Jewish involvement for this generation of bright and well-educated Jews will depend on the quality of learning and how well we communicate the

excitement of the learning process for all ages, across generational lines.

The mention of hevruta brings me to the next important area where I believe the synagogue can make a distinct contribution: the creation of intimate and caring community. Possibly the most important role that religion has to play in contemporary American society is the preservation of small face-to-face communities of people with common values and concerns. As we become ever more atomized in our lives behind our computer screens, and as "friends" turn more and more into people who see your Facebook page, real community is in sharp decline. This will be a tremendous loss on the simple human level of personal support and caring. Religious communities, especially those that still meet at least weekly, provide a true sense of connection for a large part of the American public.

Over the past several decades, partly because of the influence of the havurah movement, most liberal synagogues have moved in the direction of increasing such community-building efforts. Synagogues have become much less formal and pretentious than they were forty or fifty years ago. A sense of warmth, welcoming of newcomers, and embracing community are all values on which congregations are judged by prospective members.

Rabbis and other Jewish professionals

➤ Envisioning a Jewish Future

need to be trained in the art (yes, art, not science) of building community. HCRS places great value on the communal experience, much of it taught by personal example. The highly non-hierarchical style of student-faculty relations, as well as the sense that the faculty members themselves constitute such a community of teachers and scholars, are intentional acts of modeling from which students are meant to learn. The presence of a weekly "community time" circle, during which we all share both good and painful things happening in our personal lives, is another important model. The welcoming of new people into that community is a self-conscious and thought-out process. That sense of welcoming, of the non-hierarchical role of the rabbi, and of fostering community on every level, form a key part of our message.

Community brings me to the next important issue, that of pluralism and diversity. Because we are a pluralistic and non-denominational program, we do not have a formula to determine the right kind of Jewish living and who is a proper Jew. The synagogue of the future will need to be based on an ahavat yisra'el, love of fellow Jews, that embraces all sorts of difference. This includes difference in degrees of Jewish practice, on opinions regarding Israeli and world Jewish politics, on varying views of conversion, marriage, and divorce, differences of race, of gender definition and sexual orientation, and many more. It will also need to reach out to the sorts of Jews who would never join such an institution, including the ultra-Orthodox (this will become an increasingly difficult reach) and the avowedly secular.

Among the toughest issues our community will have to face in the decades to come is that of our relationship to Israel, including (but not limited to) the feelings aroused in liberal-oriented American Jews by Israeli government policy toward its own Arab minority and the future of the occupied territories. This problem will not go away and will not be resolved by public relations efforts or by wholesale condemnation of younger American Jews for disloyalty to the Jewish state. (I write just as the Knesset, led by the prime minister, is set to declare the precedence of "Jewish" over "democratic" in determining the state's character.) Israel must understand that its sister-community in North America is deeply committed to values of pluralistic democracy. Its desire to attract our involvement in "the state of the Jewish people" will increasingly fall on deaf ears if American Jews come to perceive Israel as a state less than fully committed to those values.

The synagogue will only attract the involvement of the coming generations if it becomes a launching pad for

➤ Envisioning a Jewish Future

enacting values that these generations respect. These include concern for the disadvantaged in all areas, both locally and internationally. Without this sense of balance and moral gravitas, the championing of exclusively Jewish concerns will seem narrowly chauvinistic, alienating increasingly large portions of a generation that may want to see itself as Jewish, but is also intimately connected to non-Jewish family members and to broader societal concerns. If "Jewish" echoes with human rights and moral responsibility, including the great questions of environmental degradation and planetary survival, the Jewish community will be respected by those it needs to attract. Without resounding commitment to these values, there is no chance.

On such matters, we are a single Jewish people. The differences between Reform, Conservative, Reconstructionist, Renewal, and large numbers of non-denominational liberal Jews (and perhaps even the Modern Orthodox, though their leaders hate to admit it) are mostly in matters of worship style and observance choices. When it comes to the issues we face as Jews in the contemporary world, our needs for building community, and the learning we seek, we are all very much the same and should be united. In this multiplex age, there is no reason that a single synagogue could not supply multiple options for worship, but have everyone join together for learning, community, hesed, and social action. The breakdown of rigid denominational lines would both provide for greater Jewish unity and save a tremendous amount of budget duplication and personal vitriol.

Finally I turn to the issue of theology, no small matter when it comes to the future of a community that is defined in mostly religious terms. What do we believe? What can we believe? Is there a way to articulate a faith for the next generation of Jews that will be at once intellectually honest, passionately exciting, and unifying? This has been my primary intellectual effort over the course of the past several decades. In the study and teaching of Hasidic and mystical sources, I have found formulations of faith that, if universalized and updated, can be re-formed into a credo that I believe can meet these criteria. You can see much of it in my neo-Hasidic credo, but more of it in *Radical Judaism* and many of my other writings. No one would be happier than I if the next generation goes ahead and improves upon what I have done, or even replaces my thinking with other forms of Judaism that share these criteria of honesty, passion, and unification. But the struggle to understand and articulate what we believe is a vital and exciting one. A rabbi is, above all, a person of vision.

➤ Envisioning a Jewish Future

To quote an old saying, "If Jews are not prophets, they are the descendants of prophets." The Jewish people needs leaders who will represent a sense of vision and faith to the communities they lead. The example of such a quest, open-ended and lifelong, is also part of the legacy that we at HCRS are giving to the future rabbis we have the great privilege to teach.

Think of the above as a program for the transformation of North American Jewish life: meaningful prayer, exciting learning, warm, inclusive community, the blurring of denominational lines, struggle with great moral issues, and an ongoing attempt at articulating a compelling vision of faith. That's what we're about in the Hebrew College Rabbinical School, and I am truly happy and proud to share this vision with you.

2025: A Post-Denominational Portrait of American Jewry

Efraim Mintz

> ➤ *Rabbi Efraim Mintz is the founding Executive Director of the Rohr Jewish Learning Institute (JLI), the largest institute of adult Jewish learning of its kind, operating 962 chapters across the globe. JLI is the adult educational arm of Chabad Lubavitch.*

Something curious happened at a recent gathering of influential philanthropists in the Jewish world. A key Jewish donor committed to progressive causes questioned her granddaughter about Jewish life at the university where she is enrolled. What Jewish group on campus, she asked – mentioning a few secular organizations by name – was her granddaughter involved with? The room was filled with a pregnant silence of disbelief when the answer came. "I'm actually involved with Chabad," replied the granddaughter.

Her response highlights a significant gap in the findings of last year's Pew Research "Portrait of Jewish Americans." The immediate take away from that expansive survey was that American Jewish life is suffering irreversible decline. Intermarriage rates are rising and community participation rates are falling. Although some 94 percent of Jews answered they were proud to be Jewish, the survey suggested that a majority are not willing to transform that feeling of pride into action.

Much of the mainstream Jewish establishment reacted to Pew's results with genuine shock and disappointment. One year later the debate continues over what course of action – if any – the Jewish community should take in the coming decade. Are the ominous conclusions arrived at by many Jewish demographers and experts correct? If so, what needs to be done to reverse, or at least slow, the trend? Which existing programs should be bolstered, and what new ideas implemented?

The Pew study has indubitably benefitted the greater Jewish community by sparking necessary, focused discussion on the challenges of Jewish continuity. As others have noted, Pew's survey was built around respondents identifying themselves as Orthodox, Conservative, Reform or just Jewish. Yet precisely because the Pew survey used this dated

➤ 2025: A Post-Denominational Portrait of American Jewry

method of self-identification in a post-denominational world, it did not take into account the true impact of Chabad on the American Jewish community. The denominational model disallows the ability to include those who participate in Chabad-Lubavitch programming while maintaining tenuous relationships with specific denominations or even totally shirking traditional labels. Had the full reach and impact of Chabad's work been properly weighed, I believe the results would have painted a far more optimistic picture of the future of American Jewry.

A Glass Half Full

While the Pew survey did not ask about Chabad participation rates, the 2014 Greater Miami Jewish Federation Population Study did, and the results showed that Chabad's message is resonating. Twenty-six percent of Miami Jews participated in Chabad activities in the last year, and, tellingly, these numbers expand greatly as you get into the younger cohort. In contrast to households led by someone 75 or over, of which ten percent participated in Chabad activities in the last year, 47 percent of households led by someone under age 35 have done so in the same time period. Forty two percent of families with children at home took part in Chabad activities in the last year. Many of these young people made

their initial connection with Chabad on university campuses, in summer camps and through youth programs, a connection they maintain as they move on with their lives and begin raising families. They also do not share some of the same kneejerk reactions that the old labeling system inculcated in past generations of American Jews. As Shmuel Rosner at the Los Angeles Jewish Journal recently surmised, "the younger generation of post denominational tendencies doesn't have the instinctive organizational objection to Chabad (ultra-Orthodox, black hat, etc.), and hence is much more willing to participate in Chabad activities without thinking too much about ideological differences."

The Miami numbers are indicative of a trend that until recently was completely overlooked. It shows that while American Jews are shirking traditional labels, the yearning for Jewish life and a deeper spiritual message is alive and well. Of Chabad's participants, only 25 percent call themselves Orthodox, while the rest identify as Conservative (32 percent), Reform (19 percent), Reconstructionist (1 percent), and most tellingly, "just Jewish" (23 percent).

Given the robustly growing reach and impact of Chabad on teenagers, college students and young professionals, American Jewry's trajectory may be far brighter than what has been suggested by Pew. In fact, as Chabad's

2025: A Post-Denominational Portrait of American Jewry

rapid rate of growth continues, more and more positions of leadership in Jewish Federations, JCCs, foundations and other Jewish non-profits, will soon be occupied by those who have been deeply affected and influenced in some way by Chabad. According to a recent California report, already some 33 percent of Jewish Federation donors are affiliated with Chabad. These numbers will only multiply as the younger generation assumes communal leadership positions.

Not long ago, a Chabad colleague of mine visited a class at the American Jewish University in Los Angeles, whose rabbinical school is affiliated with the Conservative movement. Out of 18 students in the class, 17 of them were involved in some capacity with Chabad.

Chabad has not focused on surveys, preferring to allocate precious funds toward programming and outreach. Its reliance on anecdotal evidence, however powerful, has often been cited as the reason why it has mostly been omitted from Jewish population studies. The Miami survey shows that the numbers do support much of the anecdotal evidence, which points towards participating in Chabad as a rapidly growing trend.

Around the world teenagers are joining Chabad's CTeen network, college students are connecting with Chabad on Campus and young professionals are taking part in Young Jewish Professionals' events. These young Jews are forging deep relationships and friendships with over 4,000 Chabad shluchim and shluchot stationed in virtually every Jewish community, who are carefully and strategically building a brighter Jewish future one community a time, one family at a time and one person at a time.

What the Pew survey exposed was not an American Jewish community in peril, but a Jewish leadership and establishment with restricted vision, too focused on outdated labels and existing Jewish community structures. Ten years from now, these positive communal trends that were discounted by the Jewish leadership will be looked upon with relief.

The Soul of Judaism

The vast majority of Chabad's members may not become Orthodox, nor does the local Chabad rabbi reaching out to them expect them to do so. Yet it is precisely at Chabad that these Jews, who often come from the most extreme secular backgrounds, will begin to reconnect in a meaningful way to their heritage, impacting their choices in critical matters such as marriage and how they will choose to educate their children.

So what drives Chabad's vision of a great and burgeoning American Jewish future? What is the key to Chabad's

➤ 2025: A Post-Denominational Portrait of American Jewry

success that will likely continue to grow and influence an ever widening circle of Jews from across the communal spectrum? And how might all Jewish organizations glean lessons from Chabad's success and learn from its formula?

Last month, I attended the Jewish Federations of North America's General Assembly in Washington, D.C. and heard from Jonathan Kessler, AIPAC's Leadership Development Director. He repeated a personal experience, namely how each week he would pass a young Chabad student at New York's Penn Station asking strangers if they were Jewish and offering them a chance to don tefillin. Kessler told the crowd that he himself had always declined the offer. One day he approached the young Chabadnik and asked whether he had ever found success in his work. Kessler had never witnessed anyone actually putting on tefillin, and assumed he must therefore be failing at his work. The Chabad boy replied that once in a while he did find someone who agreed to wrap the tefillin, but then he added the following:

"It depends on how you define success in my mission. My job is to stand here and let people know that there's someone out there who loves them enough to ask them whether they'd like to put on tefillin." With respect to that mission, the Chabad boy had indeed been overwhelmingly successful.

Kessler put on tefillin.

This story speaks to the true secret of Chabad's work and success.

Rabbi Schneur Zalman of Liadi, the founder of the Chabad school of thought, penned his small yet powerful magnum opus, the *Tanya*, in 1796. The book's thirty-second chapter, corresponding to the Hebrew letters lamed bet, which together spell the word lev, or heart, explicitly lays out Chabad's recipe for success. Rabbi Schneur Zalman explains that one can view the world through two different lenses: material and spiritual. If the material world remains our primary lens there is no way we can view ourselves as one cohesive Jewish community. It is only when we transcend the bodily self – the attitudes, turf and politics that divide one from another – that we can see ourselves for who we are, and subsequently our fellow Jews for who they are. At the level of the soul we are all children of God, brothers and sisters, equal parts of one larger whole.

It was the famed Baal Shem Tov who first broke convention in the eighteenth century when he began preaching that the simplest Jewish peasant folk were just as Jewish as the many great Torah scholars of the day. He taught that even the simplest Jew, one who had never engaged in any Torah study or Mitzvah observance, was just as Jewish as Moses. Torah study or Mitzvah observance has never made one more Jewish, and lack

2025: A Post-Denominational Portrait of American Jewry

of observance cannot make him less so. It is the Jewish soul that constitutes who a Jew is, and it is this message that has been the banner of Chabad to this day. It's how Chabad sees the world.

So how does Chabad's trademark loving acceptance of all Jews coincide with its goal to inspire greater Jewish observance and engagement? The answer to this seemingly practical question is necessarily metaphysical. Active Jewish engagement allows the conscious self to find its harmony, in the recesses of the psyche, with the neshamah, the soul. Thus, the loving acceptance and the simultaneous encouragement to further Jewish knowledge and observance are ironically rooted in the same philosophical cornerstone: the recognition of one's true essence. People tend not to resent being encouraged to do more when the urging stems from a recognition of who they really are, and how they can be truer to themselves. On the contrary, it reaffirms their significance – they are affirmed in a way that they know intuitively the authenticity of the appeal and the greatness of who they are and what they are called upon to be.

When it comes to caring for fellow Jews, reaching out to them and inviting them to take their rightful place in the chain of Jewish continuity, offering them the chance to put on tefillin, inviting them to a Torah class, helping them at a time of personal crisis or pouring them a hot bowl of chicken soup are all equally vital. It is the Jewish soul being touched and being granted a conduit for expression.

A Model with Greater Promise

The numbers are beginning to bear witness to the fact that this approach is not only crucial, but working.

The Lubavitcher Rebbe, Rabbi Menachem M. Schneerson, would often stress that the key to Jewish continuity lies in understanding our collective past. Ours has been a supernatural existence, one rooted in Torah study and Jewish ritual practice. The greatest human mind, however well-meaning, could not possibly formulate a remedy for what is in essence a problem of supernatural dimensions. Simply put, our heritage and our practices, our Torah and our Mitzvot, are the path to a vibrant Jewish tomorrow.

Writing about his private audience with the Rebbe in *Commentary* magazine in 1957, Herbert Weiner, himself a Reform rabbi, quotes the Rebbe as telling him: "The great fault of Conservative and Reform Judaism is not that they compromise, but that they sanctify the compromise, still the conscience, and leave no possibility for return." Chabad recognizes that Jews come from a wide variety of backgrounds, have grown up in disparate homes and have had all sorts of educations. Everyone deserves

2025: A Post-Denominational Portrait of American Jewry

respect. Nevertheless, Torah and Jewish tradition still remain a constant. Rather than making today's compromise to be the end of discussion and dynamic interaction, we need to engage our tradition more deeply and profoundly, and without any pretention of having achieved all that is possible. Shedding our self-imposed limitations is our surest strategy to a bright, thriving Jewish future.

The choice to be made by the Jewish community seems quite clear. Two roads extend into the future: one toward increased Jewish observance and study, and a second heading into eventual loss of Jewish identity. The myth of the self-preserving American Jew who is devoid of Jewish tradition and practice appears to be on the verge of extinction.

The Tipping Point

So what will the Jewish world look like in ten years? I believe we are heading toward the tipping point. A decade from now we will be living in a world where young people will be turning their backs on the path of their predecessors, not to their parents' dismay, but to their delight. Instead of attending a synagogue once or twice a year, they will be seeking to connect to their heritage daily. Synagogues, Torah study, kosher food and Jewish school attendance will be widespread.

This prediction is based not on hope

but fueled by the reality that already surrounds us. Just last year, Rabbi David Wolpe, a leading voice within the Conservative movement, wrote in the *Washington Post*: "Being an ethical person' while central to Judaism, is not uniquely Jewish. 'Fighting for social justice' while central to Judaism, is not uniquely Jewish. Wearing tefillin, praying in Hebrew, Torah study, Kashrut, Jewish communal adherence and activities — these things … are activities that keep the core of the tradition alive. As Jews have left the latter and profess the former, adherence weakens. It requires a massive, sustained and serious effort to move the etiolated Jews of good conscience to the passionate Jews of ritual involvement."

The massive, sustained and serious effort Wolpe speaks of is already underway; increasingly, individual Jewish figures from the Conservative and Reform Jewish communities are acknowledging, as Rabbi Wolpe has, that the answer to a promising Jewish future is to be found in promoting participation in Jewish tradition and rituals. With more such voices building consensus towards outreach that draws people back to the tradition, we can achieve a tipping point, the results of which will be plainly visible in 2025.

That is why Chabad holiday programs, pre-schools, adult education and synagogue services have grown in popularity. Jews want to reconnect,

2025: A Post-Denominational Portrait of American Jewry

and Chabad's message of warmth and acceptance on the one hand, and deep spirituality and authenticity on the other, resonates.

This is particularly evident in the rapid increase of Jewish adults embracing rigorous Jewish learning. The Rohr Jewish Learning Institute (JLI), Chabad's adult education arm, has witnessed monumental growth over the past decade, expanding to almost 1000 chapters around the world. These courses and seminars are not limited to one segment of the population; in addition to the flagship JLI courses, Rosh Chodesh Society caters solely to women, Sinai Scholars to students on campus, and JLI Teens to teenagers. The latter two groups correlate with the 47 percent under the age of 35 who have participated in Chabad activities in Miami. They will constitute the majority in ten years.

While the future appears to be far brighter than forecast, we should not be passive bystanders to this unfolding transformation. Each of us should endeavor to partake in this renaissance by personally growing in Jewish observance and commitment.

In 1972, Senator Frank Lautenberg, then a board member of the United Jewish Appeal (now the Jewish Federations of North America) and two years later its youngest national chair, had a wide-ranging private audience with the Rebbe. The two discussed Lautenberg's successful business, Israel, Soviet Jewry and the policies of the UJA. Then discussion turned to Lautenberg's personal life, and the Rebbe encouraged him to grow in his Judaism, increase his observance of Mitzvot, and to begin putting on tefillin. As the meeting came to an end, the Rebbe looked at Lautenberg and told him:

"If you will look in the mirror tomorrow morning and you will see the same Lautenberg as yesterday – that means I have achieved nothing."

"You achieved plenty, plenty," replied Lautenberg.

"That all depends on you," the Rebbe told him.

The old system of boxing Jews into predefined categories has failed us. There is a positive future for American

JEWISH LEARNING INSTITUTE

2025: A Post-Denominational Portrait of American Jewry

Jewry, but it all depends on continuing to break the barriers that have until now divided us, from each other and from our own selves. As we come home to ourselves today, we unlock an incredibly bright tomorrow.

The Orthodox Rabbinate and its Chabad Revolution

Zev Eleff

> ➤ *Rabbi Dr. Zev Eleff has written more than a dozen scholarly articles on American Jewish history and Orthodox Judaism.*

In November 2014, the Young Israel of Phoenix elected Rabbi Yossi Bryski to serve as its spiritual leader. The Chabad-trained rabbi had earned a fine reputation for his work as an adult educator in nearby Scottsdale. His efforts more than impressed Young Israel's lay leaders, who acknowledged that it is "uncommon" for Modern Orthodox congregations to look to Chabad to fill pulpit vacancies in American synagogues. Nonetheless, the Phoenix congregation hired the talented Bryski, despite his lack of familiarity with more mainstream American Orthodox prayer book and religious sensibilities.[1]

In fact, what happened in the Young Israel of Phoenix is not an all-too-peculiar occurrence.[2] In recent years, a number of North American Orthodox congregations have hired Chabad extracts to lead their non-Chabad synagogues. The list includes Congregation Beth Tefillah of Atlanta, Beit David Highland Lakes Shul of Aventura, B'nai Ruven of Chicago, Young Israel of Lawrenceville, Congregation Shaarei Tefila of Los Angeles, Skylake Synagogue of Miami, Congregation Chevra Kadisha of Montreal, Congregation Ahavath Chesed of New London, Palm Beach Synagogue, Congregation B'nai Jacob of Park Slope, Vilna Congregation and B'nai Abraham of Philadelphia, Ahavath Torah of Short Hills, Kehillat Shaarei Torah of Toronto and Congregation Shevet Achim of Seattle.[3] In some of these cases, congregations suffering diminished membership invited Chabad to assume control in an attempt to revive local religious life. In others, Orthodox laypeople viewed Chabad-educated clergymen as better candidates than other seminary-schooled rabbis to serve their "Modern Orthodox" communities.

Of course, the majority of Orthodox congregations hire non-Chabad clergymen. Still, Chabad's influence on the broader Orthodox rabbinate is significant.[4] Rabbis and laypeople encounter Chabad emissaries in

The Orthodox Rabbinate and its Chabad Revolution

their extended communities with variant visions of congregational life. Orthodox Judaism is sometimes at odds with the more particular Chabad brand. For example, the rank-and-file Orthodox Jews in the United States support local (non-Chabad) day schools and a general synthesis of Judaism and Western culture. In turn, laypeople expect that their rabbis relay these sentiments in their own actions and sermons, oftentimes with a proof-text from the writings of the late Rabbi Joseph B. Soloveitchik of Yeshiva University.[5] In contrast, Chabad rabbis prefer to lecture on "Jewish values" and concentrate on Jewish outreach to unaffiliated coreligionists. Moreover, they favor tales and pithy lessons of their Hassidic masters rather than high-brow rabbinic ideologues.

In response, rabbis of all stripes voice displeasure over Chabad's penetration into "foreign sectors" of American Judaism. Some focus on the messianic culture that surrounds its late leader, Rabbi Menachem Mendel Schneerson. Others accuse Chabad of diluting sophisticated Jewish experiences with trite messages and simple teachings. A Reform leader once quipped that Chabad "is the place that you go when you do not want to join a synagogue or subject your child to a meaningful course of study."[6] In 2007, a Jew in Morristown, New Jersey, criticized Chabad for "short-circuiting the Jewish

experience to achieve their goal of saving Jewish souls."[7]

Others are more sanguine. They credit Chabad for their patience and ability to foster relationships, with concurring and dissimilar Jews alike. "Chabad's success is largely predicated on the cardinal community organization principle," opined a well-connected American Jew. "The monumental advantage Chabad engenders is that their emissaries truly, really, unequivocally love Jews."[8] A leading Conservative rabbi concurred: "One of the things that we can learn from Chabad: I think they really understood sooner than others the importance of building personal relationships. Much of Chabad's success is built on personal relationships."[9]

To insiders, the Orthodox consternation is noticeable but very much suppressed. Overall, its leaders do not issue overt criticism of their Chabad challengers. Instead, Orthodox rabbis choose to emulate them. Perhaps, much of the similarities between Chabad and current trends within the Orthodox rabbinate are mostly correlative rather than causative. The alternative is suggestive but difficult to prove (though, I will try anyway). After all, the same ecumenical and moralistic forces that have empowered Chabad also enable the efforts of conservative Protestant groups.[10] Nevertheless, the present class of rabbis takes note

The Orthodox Rabbinate and its Chabad Revolution

of the "band of ragtag rabbis" that— despite their unkempt beards—attract Sabbath worshipers and manage to fundraise better than possibly any other American Jewish movement.[11] For the Orthodox rabbinate, then, it is a matter of keeping pace.

The Present-Day Orthodox Pastor

In 1988, Rabbi Sherman Kirshner issued a complaint about the American rabbinate. As a member of Hebrew Theological College's rabbinic placement committee, the Michigan-based rabbi had learned much about the expectations of Orthodox congregations. "Never was there mention made of the candidate's inability to preach effectively, to conduct a class for adults or youngsters, or perform any of the rabbinical duties normally expected," explained Kirshner. "Rather," he confessed, laypeople "complain of a gross lack of understanding between personalities." To this writer's mind, there was a great need for rabbis to gain expert training in pastoral counseling. "It will prove invaluable to them," asserted Kirshner, "in their daily dealings with community members, and to understand them better and to counsel effectively."[12] Since then, other Orthodox schools and institutions have redoubled their efforts to enable Orthodox rabbis to address the social and mental-health needs of their congregants. In 1999,

Rabbi Avi Weiss founded Yeshivat Chovevei Torah in part to train rabbis with a greater concern for the pastoral areas of the profession. In addition, Yeshiva University and National Council of Young Israel have retooled their programs to educate rabbinical students and rabbis to better counsel laypeople.[13]

To some extent, Orthodox Judaism's latter-day emphasis on pastoral training represents its attempt to catch up to other Jewish enclaves and their rabbinical schools. Yet, the leader of this so-called "Relational Judaism" is Chabad. This is how one astute observer put it:

"In a nutshell, the Chabad rabbi knows how to build warm, personal relationships, beginning with a nonjudgmental welcome and a personal invitation to share a meal in his home. And, once you're in a relationship with a Chabad rabbi, he knows your name, he is at your side when stuff happens in your life, he is usually a good teacher, and he empowers you Jewishly. Yes, he is an aggressive fundraiser, but people give because they are grateful for the relationship."[14]

More to the point, the Chabad rabbinate is fundamentally pastoral, despite that its students receive minimal professional training. The rabbis who represent this Hassidic movement are taught that an easygoing and non-judgmental demeanor is

The Orthodox Rabbinate and its Chabad Revolution

critical to accomplish their sacred task of outreach. This style suits the women and men with whom Chabad interacts. These Jews much prefer a Judaism that can be understood without extensive Jewish literacy and offered to them by a warm and indulgent pastor. It is also conceivable that the many unaffiliated Jews who enter "Chabad houses" also enjoy that their local rabbi is a Lubavitch hassid with the otherworldliness trappings of a long beard and coat rather than a well-groomed Orthodox rabbi dressed in a standard suit and tie. Years ago, this style and outreach objective did not interest the American Orthodox clergyman. He preferred a "formal look" and was content with "in-reach," appealing to the steadfast Orthodox Jews while permitting the rest to winnow away into secular or non-Orthodox sectors.[15] This situation is now altogether altered. Notwithstanding the Old World attire, the Modern Orthodox rabbi follows in his Chabad rival's somewhat-eccentric path. He too aims to concretize Jewish learning into more digestible forms. He embraces the non-Orthodox and the not-too-Orthodox Jew as a chance to draw them closer to his way of life.

The consequence of this shift is in some ways quite severe. By and large, the Orthodox rabbinate has moved away from the intellectualism that marked its "high point" in the 1960s.[16] Today, the leading scholars of Orthodox Judaism are accused of "abdicating critical thinking for sermonizing" and engaging in "logical fallacies" and presenting "ahistorical assumptions as fact."[17] Though harsh, the evaluation is on target. The number of Orthodox journals is down from decades ago. The books and articles produced by exponents of Orthodox Judaism lack the heft and depth of yesteryear. The rational intellectual vibe once championed by Orthodox scholars has at present given way to a "growing trend among the Modern Orthodox to reconnect with the spiritual vision of the Ba'al Shem Tov and his disciples and others who delved into this dimension of Torah."[18]

Overall, though, laypeople have welcomed this new breed. Before the 1980s, it was a rare occurrence when a rabbinic search committee included pastoral work in its request for applications. They might have expected it, but counseling was not high on laypeople's lists. This has changed, however. In recent years, a New York congregation required that its pulpit vacancy be filled by someone competent in "key areas of organizational life: spiritual, counseling and membership development." In California, a search committee indicated that it strongly wanted to hire someone with pastoral skills over a candidate with outstanding teaching or preaching abilities. In 1994, a social

The Orthodox Rabbinate and its Chabad Revolution

worker with deep knowledge of the Orthodox community concluded that "the rabbi is a key person in regard to whether or not Orthodox emotionally disturbed persons will seek and receive mental health services."[19] Two years ago, an internal survey of an Orthodox congregation in New England found that most members valued a rabbi's "communication skills" and ability to provide pastoral counseling more than his ability to deliver a sermon or determine matters of Jewish law.

The change is apparent beyond the synagogue pulpit, as well. Consider the transformation of the National Conference of Synagogue Youth. In 1954, leaders of the Orthodox Union founded NCSY to serve as a social conduit for Orthodox youngsters. For scores of traditional-minded young people in Savannah, for example, the youth movement offered them a "sense of belonging."[20] Far from an outreach organization, NCSY in its first decades networked likeminded Orthodox youth in a period in which most Orthodox children did not have access to Orthodox high schools.[21] The current condition of NCSY is much different, and now in line with the Chabad outreach mission. Rather than reinforce the Orthodox establishment, the youth organization's rabbinic advisors and administrators mostly target non-observant Jewish youngsters. Most often, the Orthodox-

fortified teenagers involved in NCSY see it as their role to model Orthodox behavior for their religiously-at-risk counterparts.

Furthermore, the standard educational fare taught and distributed through NCSY has also undergone considerable adjustment. In its earliest years, the national organization published newspapers and books that offered young readers thoughtful and text-based ideas. In the 1970s, the effort was spearheaded by Rabbi Aryeh Kaplan, who possessed a skill for explaining complicated ideas in a readable manner.[22] This is no longer the case. The current NCSY output features tales extracted from Hassidic lore and well-packaged messages that speak to "Jewish values." The minority of Orthodox Jews who lament this development echoes the complaints lodged against Chabad. "NCSY has won," bemoaned an observer. "It has replaced shiurim [lectures] in our community's intellectual life. Of course it has, it requires little effort and makes you feel good, too."[23]

The Orthodox Rabbi's Wife

In 1990, Fay Kranz declared the Chabad rebbetzin a "minor miracle." The writer surmised that the Chabad rabbi's wife had become "an integral part of the organization and her husband could not function without her."[24] The position of the Chabad

The Orthodox Rabbinate and its Chabad Revolution

rebbetzin cannot be understated. At the minimum, she runs the preschools and other educational activities which help bring children and their parents into the Chabad fold. In truth, though, her position is far more essential to the Chabad cause. Paired with her unshaven unmodern-seeming husband, the standard Chabad rebbetzin is sure to appear in public covered with heavy doses of makeup and clothed in stylish outfits. For many Orthodox and non-Orthodox Jews, it is the Chabad woman who is far more approachable and relatable to their modern senses. The rebbetzin, therefore, is more than a vital component of the Chabad organization: she is a full-partner in the Chabad enterprise. For sure, there are limits. The rebbetzin does not lead prayer services. Yet, cloaked in a traditional role, the female emissary heads many of the Chabad events and functions in areas that her husband is too socially limited to properly access.[25]

Likewise, the mainstream Orthodox rebbetzin has also secured a stronger foothold in congregational life. For years, Orthodox laypeople saddled the rabbi's wife with a myriad of responsibilities, but most centered on her responsibility as a hostess.[26] This, too, has changed. Moreover, in contrast to the ongoing efforts to train women to serve as Orthodox clergy, the "New Role for Rebbetzins" has not encountered resistance.[27] In 1998, Abby

Lerner of the Young Israel of Great Neck submitted that in her station as the congregation's first lady, she acts as educator and pastoral caregiver and resource on matters of Jewish law.[28] While Lerner was careful to couch her powers in most traditional and feminine terms, her list of clerical responsibilities resembles the portfolio of Orthodox rabbis, notwithstanding the latter's more visible participation in public worship. Accordingly, the Modern Orthodox and Chabad rebbetzins have managed to enlarge their role while operating within the patriarchal arena of their rabbinic husbands.

The rising stature of the rebbetzin in congregational life is sometimes taken for granted. "It should not go unsaid," wrote Yocheved Goldberg of Boca Raton Synagogue, "that in almost every single Jewish community, there already is a woman in a position of great leadership who helps shape the vision and agenda of the community, who has full access to the rabbi and is uninhibited to speak with him freely: the Rebbetzin."[29] Like Abby Lerner before her, this writer was careful to circumscribe her "leadership" in "Orthodox" language: she itemized her responsibilities that included study-sessions with bat mitzvah girls, brides and conversion candidates. Despite no formal training, Goldberg also felt it within her purview to "teach classes, field questions, host people at our

➤ The Orthodox Rabbinate and its Chabad Revolution

Shabbos and Yom Tov [holiday] tables and partner with our husbands in leading the community."[30]

Of course, there are degrees of traditionalism in the rebbetzin's rhetoric. In Edmonton, another rabbi's wife voiced little doubt about the extent of her clerical responsibilities. To this rebbetzin, proof of her rabbinical credentials derived from her standing with the Rabbinical Council of America as well as the more-or-less accurate description of contemporary Orthodox rabbinic placement:

"What category do rebbetzins fall under? Are we not part of the Orthodox rabbinate? Let's be honest. The RCA certainly recognizes the role of rebbetzins. We are all invited to attend the RCA annual conventions and there are even separate rebbetzins' sessions. So how could they issue such a statement? The Orthodox rabbinate entails a partnership of rabbi and rebbetzin. There is no Orthodox shul today that will hire a single rabbi, i.e. a rabbi without a rebbetzin. There is an unwritten two-for-one deal; indeed, some shuls even go as far as to place expectations on the rebbetzin in the job description, all the while stating that they are just hiring a rabbi!"[31]

Truth to tell, Batya Ivry-Friedman of Edmonton's Beth Israel Synagogue has a point. Routinely, the advertisements for pulpit positions ask for "active" or "engaging" rebbetzins who will pledge to contribute to synagogue culture. In some instances, search committees respect the right of the rabbi's wife to concentrate on her career or focus on her children. Yet, it is more and more the case that congregations search for a husband and wife to serve as a rabbinic couple.

This is certainly true for the Orthodox Union's Jewish Learning Initiative on Campus program. Now a part of Jewish life on twenty-one North American campuses, JLIC places rabbinic couples in Hillel settings to support Orthodox collegians. While the duties of the JLIC rebbetzin can vary, the OU requires that the female "co-director" serves on a part time basis. The parallel between the JLIC couple and the Chabad rabbi and rebbetzin on college campuses is unmistakable. "In many ways," noted one observer. "JLIC is similar to Chabad's on-campus program: Both send a young rabbi and wife, who open their homes to students as well as providing a wide range of Torah classes, rabbinic services and personal outreach."[32]

No doubt, a number of factors contribute to this condition. On the whole, sisterhoods and ladies auxiliaries have disappeared from the synagogue infrastructure. In turn, the active rebbetzin has replaced these erstwhile important organizations to fill the famine void in the synagogue. In addition, the decision in Reform

The Orthodox Rabbinate and its Chabad Revolution

(1972) and Conservative Judaism (1984) to ordain women as rabbis and continued agitation to do the same in the Orthodox realm have moved Orthodox Jews to push the traditional-appearing rebbetzin into a more visible position.[33] Still, the concomitant rise of the Chabad rabbinate and its female accompaniment in the United States cannot be overlooked. "I think there's a lot to learn from Chabad, to be honest," admitted an Agudath Israel leader in 2003. In that interview, Rabbi Avi Shafran specifically referred to the Chabad efforts in outreach, which to his mind, "has, over recent decades, become very much part of the mainstream stance of mainstream Orthodox American Judaism."[34] As a matter of fact, Chabad's influence is much more than that.

(Endnotes)

I dutifully offer my gratitude to Yitzi Ehrenberg, Yair Sturm, Shimon Unterman and Shlomo Zuckier for their very helpful comments on an earlier draft of this article.

1 See Leisah Woldoff, "Shifts Occur in Phoenix's Orthodox Community," Jewish News (November 14, 2014): 2.

2 See Sue Fishkoff, The Rebbe's Army: Inside the World of Chabad-Lubavitch (New York: Schocken Books, 2003), 111.

3 I generated this far from exhaustive list with the help of the Wexner Graduate Fellow and Alumni list-serv. I thank those who responded to my query with examples of Chabad-trained rabbis in non-Chabad

Orthodox congregations.

4 See Adam S. Ferziger, "From Lubavitch to Lakewood: The Chabadization of American Orthodoxy," Modern Judaism 33 (May 2013): 101-24.

5 See Lawrence Grossman, "Modern Orthodoxy's Human Pillar," Forward (September 2, 2011): 9.

6 See Andrew Silow-Carroll, "Chabad Influence," New Jersey Jewish News (November 8, 2007): 4.

7 "Chabad Influence—the Readers' Turn," New Jersey Jewish News (November 22, 2007): 4.

8 Ibid.

9 Bryan Schwartzman, "Chabad Influence," Inside 34 (Spring & Summer 2013): 37.

10 See Paul Boyer, "The Evangelical Resurgence in the 1970s: American Protestantism," in Rightward Bound: Making America Conservative in the 1970s, eds. Bruce J. Schulman and Julian E. Zelizer (Cambridge: Harvard University Press, 2008), 34-35; and Darren Dochuk, From Bible Belt to Sunbelt: Plain Folk Religion, Grassroots Politicians, and the Rise of Evangelical Conservatism (New York: W.W. Norton, 2011), 326-61.

11 See, for example, Dovid Efune, "Chabad is Scrappy and Disorganized—So Why Do Donors Love it?," Jewish News Weekly of Southern California (November 19, 2010): 28.

12 Sherman P. Kirshner, "Needed: Clinical Pastoral Training," Jewish Spectator 53 (Fall 1988): 63.

13 See Zev Eleff, "From Teach to Scholar to Pastor: The Evolving Postwar Modern Orthodox Rabbinate," American Jewish History 98 (October 2014): 308-13.

The Orthodox Rabbinate and its Chabad Revolution

14 Ron Wolfson, *Relational Judaism: Using the Power of Relationships to Transform the Jewish Community* (Woodstock, VT: Jewish Lights Publishing, 2013), 88

15 See Jeffrey S. Gurock, "The Winnowing of American Orthodoxy," in *Approaches to Modern Judaism*, vol. II (Chico: Scholars Press, 1984), 41-53.

16 See Jonathan Sacks, *Future Tense: Jews, Judaism, and Israel in the Twenty-First Century* (New York: Schocken Books, 2009), 210.

17 Michael Nutkiewicz, "Sacks' Sermon?," *Jewish Review of Books* 5 (Fall 2014): 4.

18 Barbara Bensoussan, "Rekindling the Flame: Neo-Chassidus Brings the Inner Light of Torah to Modern Orthodoxy," *Jewish Action* 75 (Winter 2014): 22.

19 Eleff, "From Teacher to Scholar to Pastor," 312.

20 Abraham I. Rosenberg to Samuel Belkin, December 18, 1956, Box 14, Folder: "Georgia, Savannah—Cong. B'nai B'rith Jacob," YU Rabbinic Placement Records, Yeshiva University Archives, New York, NY.

21 See Zev Eleff, *Living from Convention to Convention: A History of the NCSY, 1954-1980* (Jersey City: Ktav, 2009).

22 Ibid., 61-72.

23 Yitzchak Talansky, "Naaseh V'nishma," *Klal Perspectives* 1 (Summer 2012): 166.

24 Fay Kranz, "The Super Shlicha," in *Shlichus: Meeting the Outreach Challenge*, ed. Chana Piekarski (Brooklyn: Nshei Chabad Publications, 1990), 19.

25 See Naftali Loewenthal, "From 'Ladies' Auxiliary' to 'Shluhot Network': Women's Activism in Twentieth Century Habad," in *A Touch of Grace: Studies in Ashkenazi Culture, Women's History, and the Languages of the Jews Presented to Chava Turniansky*, eds. Israel Bartal et al. (Jerusalem: The Zalman Shazar Center for Jewish History, 2013), 69-93. See also Bonnie J. Morris, *Lubavitcher Women in America: Identity and Activism in the Postwar Era* (Albany: State University of New York Press, 1998), 105; and Elite Ben-Yosef, "Literacy and Power: The Shiyour as a Site of Subordination and Empowerment for Chabad Women," *Journal of Feminist Studies in Religion* 27 (Spring 2011): 53-74.

26 See, for example, Helen Felman, "A Rebitzen Respectfully Dissents," *Chavrusa* 4 (November 1959): 5. For a historical overview of the rebbetzin profession, see Shuly Rubin Schwartz, *The Rabbi's Wife: The Rebbetzin in American Jewish Life* (New York: New York University Press, 2006).

27 On this, see Darren Kleinberg, "Orthodox Women (Non-)Rabbis," *CCAR Journal* 59 (Spring 2012): 80-99.

28 See Abby Lerner, "New Roles of Rebbetzins: Teacher, Halachic Liaison, Counselor, & Friend," *Rebbetzin's Letter* (Summer 1998): 3

29 Yocheved Goldberg, "A Good Reason Not to Lose Faith in the Rabbinate—the Rebbetzins," *Rabbi's Blog*, November 14, 2014, http://rabbisblog.brsonline.org/good-reason-lose-faith-rabbinate-rebbetzins/.

30 Ibid. In an earlier essay, Goldberg admitted that her station was earned through marriage; she did not undergo requisite training for her unpaid but prominent role in her community. See Yocheved Goldberg, "The Rebbetzin's Juggling Act," *Rabbi's Blog*, January 11, 2013, http://rabbisblog. brsonline.org/the-rebbetzins-juggling-act/.

31 Batya Ivry-Friedman, "Should We Invite Maharats to the Rebbetzins Conference?,"

➤ The Orthodox Rabbinate and its Chabad Revolution

Times of Israel Blog, November 17, 2014, http://blogs.timesofisrael.com/maharats-and-rebbetzins/.

32 Sue Fishkoff, "Reaching Out to Orthodox Students," *Jewish Telegraphic Agency,* November 15, 2005.

33 See Pamela S. Nadell, *Women Who Would Be Rabbis: A History of Women's Ordination, 1889-1985 (Boston: Beacon Press, 1998)*

34 Uriel Heilman, "Chabad's Model of Outreach Gains Favor Among Fervently Orthodox," *Jewish Telegraphic Agency,* December 11, 2003.

Like Sheep Without a Shepherd

Martin S. Cohen

➤ **Rabbi Martin S. Cohen** *is the rabbi of the Shelter Rock Jewish Center in Roslyn, New York, and can be reached at rabbi@srjc.org.*

Lacking a crystal ball, I propose we begin to consider what the Jewish world will be like ten years' hence by engaging that peculiar Jewish ability to look forwards by looking backwards, thus to see what lies ahead by studying terrain already covered and allowing what we know of the road travelled to suggest something about the road yet to come. I will leave to other contributors to this journal to discuss issues that loom large on the horizon but regarding which I have no particular expertise. Instead, I would like to propose an idea for my readers' consideration that I do know all about, one that seems to me to rest at the heart of the matter as I personally wonder what will befall the House of Israel in the coming years.

When I allow myself to make my own experiences the lens through which the past is projected into the future, I see a Jewish world characterized by a crippling lack of leadership, one that more than anything else resembles Moses' worst nightmare for his people as he spoke from the very edge of his own life and begged God to send someone worthy to replace him lest the people be "like sheep that have no shepherd" (Number 27:17). God, touched by Moses' dying wish that he be replaced by someone able and willing to accept the mantle of national leadership, instantly instructs Moses to transfer the charisma of leadership to Joshua both formally by placing his hands upon him in public and also by transferring to Joshua some of his own majestic bearing. (How exactly Moses is to do that is left unexplained. Rashi, commenting ad locum, suggests that the idea was for Moses to project some of the light radiating out from his effulgent face onto Joshua and that that would do the trick. It would be interesting to know if Rashi was right. But surely the more important point is that Moses apparently understood what was being asked of him, not that we do not.) This is not to say that there are no Jewish leaders in the world; rather, it is true Jewish leadership, with all the charisma and gravitas that it should

➤ Like Sheep Without a Shepherd

and can entail, that has been lost.

When I was a student at the Jewish Theological Seminary in the 1970s, the Jewish world was home to any number of individuals who were universally recognized, including by people who differed with them (and who even disagreed with them vehemently) about specific issues, as leaders of the American Jewish community. The people of whom I am thinking were very different in many ways, but what they all had in common was the foundation of deep cultural awareness and learning upon which they stood. These were leaders so fully and absolutely steeped in Jewish culture and Jewish learning that it seems hard to imagine them in any other context at all: despite the famous, oft-cited comment by Solomon Schechter about the indispensable need for American rabbis to know all about baseball, it is as hard for me to imagine Louis Finkelstein actually taking up softball in his spare time—and I speak as someone who served as the man's research assistant for most of my years at JTS—as it would be to imagine Menachem Schneerson bowling or Joseph Soloveitchik playing miniature golf.

Am I falling prey to the "golden age" syndrome, that particular version of craziness that makes people my age imagine that things were invariably better in the good old days of their irretrievable youths? I suppose we must all consider that possibility when we find ourselves looking backwards wistfully, but it doesn't feel that way to me. Just to the contrary, actually, is how it feels: we live in a Jewish world in which people with almost no Jewish learning at all claim—and to a great extent succeed at assuming—significant positions of Jewish leadership.

As far as I can see, no member of the Conference of Presidents of Major American Jewish Organizations could possibly claim to be a leader of American Jewry, let alone world Jewry, in that sense of the word I have in mind. Nor can the current leadership of any Jewish seminary in the United States seriously claim to speak on behalf of American Jewry in a way even remotely comparable to the way Maimonides represented Egyptian Jewry in his day. Nor do we have leaders who can give a thoughtful response fully steeped in the Jewish tradition to social injustice in the same way that Abraham Joshua Heschel could in his day: when Heschel marched at Selma with Martin Luther King Jr., for example, he was widely and reasonably understood to be the living embodiment of his people in his adopted country, living proof that Jewry can rise above particularistic politics while still being fully entrenched in tradition. It is precisely that kind of leadership that we lack, the kind entrusted to leaders who are learned, suffused totally with Jewishness,

Like Sheep Without a Shepherd

possessed of the deepest understanding of tradition acquired through a lifetime of intensive study, and able to command the respect of others not by demanding it but by inspiring it through piety, erudition, faith, absolute intellectual and spiritual integrity, and the deepest and most abiding allegiance to Jewish observance.

What will happen if we continue to steer forward the ship without captains at the helm able to guide us towards a future in which Jews everywhere feel inspired eagerly to embrace their Jewishness and their Judaism seems obvious: the ship will sail around endlessly in ever-wider, ever-less-goal-driven circles and eventually flounder on the shoals of irrelevance. When I project the contemporary view ten years into the future and see the Jewish world even more unraveled and unstable than it is today because of a lack of true, commanding leadership at the top, I feel despondent. And, rationally speaking, why shouldn't I? Nor can we rationally hope to import leadership from elsewhere, like the American Jewish community did in the past. Indeed, what American Jewry needs today is an indigenous revitalization, specifically not one brought in from the outside.

From where will these leaders emerge? One of the foundational ideas of North American culture is the notion of limitless merit-based opportunity. There is a certain satisfying republicanism to the notion that anyone can grow up to be president, and that all that is required to be a great leader is initiative, here defined as the mere desire to step forward and successfully to assume the mantle of leadership. But embedded in that set of ideas is a less-noticed corollary: that, because leaders following this paradigm step forward from the people, there must inevitably be a certain commonality that links the leader to the led. Taken one step further we come to the notion that to be a leader one not only may, but actually must, be cut from the same cloth as those one guides forward and, indeed, the primus inter pares model supports that concept by suggesting that one can indeed be of the people and over them at the same time. This model works in the Supreme Court of the United States, for example, where the Chief Justice presides over the court and has distinctive administrative responsibilities but no actual control over the opinions, legal and otherwise, of the other justices, thus being over the other justices and of them at the same time. To work well in the American Jewish context, however, this concept needs serious adjustment. In fact, this notion, so current in the Jewish world that it feels almost axiomatic in most contexts, is part of our problem: having not been at all careful regarding that for which we wished, we have been granted

Like Sheep Without a Shepherd

leaders who are just larger, richer, more forceful, and/or more powerful versions of ourselves. But that is not at all where we should have gone or where we should go as we make our way through the next decade and come out, either better or less well off, at the other end in 2025. Obviously, our leaders must be of us. Yet, our leaders must also hold to a higher moral and social standard, one that emphasizes their distinctiveness from the people they serve rather than their similarity to them. That is the reality we should demand for ourselves as we venture into the next decade.

Scripture actually has quite a bit to say about the qualities we should demand from our leaders. To return to that passage cited above, the one in which Moses pleads with God that the Israelites not be left after his death as sheep without a shepherd—I started halfway through the story without setting the words I cited in their literary context. God instructs Moses to climb a certain mountain, one called in this passage Mount Avarim, and to gaze from there at the Promised Land for it is there, atop that specific mountain that he, Moses, is going to die. And it is then, before climbing to his death, that Moses utters the prayer cited in part above "May the Eternal, God of the spirits of all flesh, appoint a leader over the community, one who will go out before them and who will come in after them, who will personally lead

them forward and oversee their return. And thus shall the congregation of the Eternal not be as sheep who have no shepherd." The leader is therefore to be someone apart from the general populace, from amkha…but also someone who will lead them out and bring them back not as the first among equals but as someone wholly distinct and different. Moses' own story is instructive: he begins living among the people, but eventually sets his tent outside the camp not because he was too good to live in the midst of the people, but in order to maintain distance from them and to model the kind of austere bearing that he no doubt hoped would adequately bear witness to the fact that Moses was chosen by God and personally invested with the divine spirit that he eventually bequeathed to his successor, to Joshua.

The text says this explicitly, by the way, noting that Joshua was an ish asheir ru·aḥ bo, a man in whom inhered the spirit of the living God, presumably in a way that set him apart from the rest of humanity. And this is also what Scripture means to teach us at 1 Samuel 10:6 when it depicts Samuel explaining to the young Saul that the sign that he, Saul, has been chosen to be king of Israel will be when he encounters a group of prophets descending from the bamah at Givat Ha-elohim and, as the spirit of God envelops and transforms him, he becomes an ish aḥeir, a different

Like Sheep Without a Shepherd

man: different from the man he was previously, but also different from the people he is now called upon to lead.

Leadership like this is not limited to Scripture. Rabbi Judah ben Shimon, the Jewish Patriarch of Roman Palestine in the second and early third centuries CE popularly called Judah the Patriarch (or, less often, Judah the Prince), was such a man in his day. And so was Samuel ibn Naghrillah, more often called Shmuel Ha-nagid by Jewish moderns, in eleventh-century Spain. Certainly, the quintessential embodiment of this kind of leadership was Maimonides himself, a man who was as deeply involved in the political landscape of his day as he was in the practice of medicine yet who nonetheless exemplified (and even today continues to exemplify) Jewish learning at its deepest and most intellectually compelling. There have been Shabbetai Tzvi's, to be sure—charlatans whose sole claim to leadership was their personal will to self-aggrandize. But there have also been Menasseh ben Israels, Moses Mendelssohns, and Rav Kooks. All lived within the four ells of halakhah, yet also managed somehow to inhabit the entire Jewish world of their day, thus to symbolize the finest and most noble spirit of Jewishness not by hiding from the world but by living fully and really in it. That should be our model for leadership, and we should, in my opinion, have the courage to establish

our hierarchy of leadership in direct proportion to the degree to which our would-be leaders approach that specific ideal.

We have manufactured a Jewish world for ourselves in these United States that shows no particular interest in denying positions of prominence to people for whom Judaism itself is only an ancillary feature of their Jewishness, and who themselves are Jewishly unlettered. To say that this will not lead us forward to a good place is to say the very least. When I look into the future and force myself to open my eyes, what I see is the national embodiment of the psalmist's self-deprecating image of himself that closes the 119th psalm, the image of himself as a lost lamb hoping against hope that he might find some way to survive in a world wholly unsympathetic to lambs and their needs.

As he faced his last hours, Moses prayed to God, and God sent Joshua to lead forward the House of Israel in Moses' stead. In a world that seems unable to distinguish between fanaticism and piety, between know-nothing fundamentalism and spiritual integrity, between self-absorption and selflessness, and between grandiosity and true leadership skills, perhaps we too should resort to prayer and hope that we not be forced to live as sheep without a shepherd, as lost lambs longing for salvation but without any

➤ Like Sheep Without a Shepherd

clear idea how or whence redemption might yet come.

I write, as I said above, as myself: as a rabbi who has devoted almost his entire professional life to service in the congregational rabbinate. Can rabbis give up their endless internecine sniping long enough to offer the Jewish world the kind of leadership it so sorely lacks? I'd like to think so. And, in fact, I do think so. Denominationalism is not quite as passé, let alone dead, as is so often advertised: as Mark Twain said of himself, the rumors of its death have been, to say the least, greatly exaggerated. But some of the bitterness that denominationalism has brought to the rabbinic enterprise has strained away, I believe, in the last decade; I am personally involved in a start-up publishing venture that has succeeded in bringing together well over 180 authors, the large majority of them rabbis, from every corner of the Jewish world to work together on books of essays intended to inspire and enthuse the larger Jewish world out there. So perhaps from that vast sea of learning can emerge leaders able to inspire and to lead, to teach and to guide forward, to stand personally for the finest Jewish values and to represent Jewishness at its finest and most stirring to the great world out there and to the men and women of Jewish America. Stranger things have happened!

Chabad has made a kind of strange virtue out of leaderlessness, just as the Breslover hasidim did before them. But although that seems to work well for both those groups, it will not serve a people as disparate and given over to querulousness and almost fetishistic disunity as contemporary American Jewry. Such a group needs a Rambam—a Maimonides—at its helm, a leader whose political acumen, spiritual bearing, rabbinic learning, intellectual integrity, emotional maturity, and moral excellence makes it unnecessary for him or her actually to campaign for the (non-existent) position of American exilarch. Can such a person step forward and seize the mantle of national, let alone trans-national, Jewish leadership in a way that brings together rather than drives apart…and in so doing makes membership in the House of Israel deeply attractive to a new generation of young people? In my opinion, the answer to that specific question more than anything else will shape American Jewry in 5785.

What Will American Jewry Look Like in 10 years?

Elana Maryles Sztokman

➤ **Dr. Elana Maryles Sztokman** is an award-winning author, educator, speaker and consultant specializing in Jewish feminism. Two of her books have won the National Jewish Book Council award. Her most recent book is The War on Women in Israel: A story of religious radicalism and the women fighting for freedom, available on Amazon. She blogs at www.jewfem.com

The American Jewish community recently experienced a new traumatic rabbinic event: An Orthodox rabbi in Washington, D.C., Barry Freundel was arrested for spying on women through hidden cameras in the mikveh (ritual bath). What followed was a swift and sonorous communal outcry that went beyond Freundel – women sharing the vulnerability of the entire mikveh experience; converts speaking out about humiliations involved in the conversion process; Orthodox rabbis practically begging their constituents not to be blamed or lumped into the same category as the voyeur. None of the issues raised was exactly new, but perhaps they were heeded in some corners of the community for the first time, or responded to with the seriousness that they deserve.

This series of events led to a few more firsts: The RCA announced that the first woman, Dr. Michelle Friedman, will be joining the board; several Orthodox opinion-makers publicly challenged the practice of men being present at the ritual immersion of female converts; and, despite years or decades in which the Israeli rabbinate made life miserable for converts and American rabbis from all denominations by picking and choosing whose conversions to accept, they announced that it would unilaterally accept all of Freundel's conversions. Freundel, it seems was not only peeping on converts. He was also representing the American Jewish community by holding secret negotiations with the Chief Rabbis over whose conversions would be accepted in Israel. The grand irony of this episode, of course, is that the ugly urgency created by Freundel's behavior opened the door wide for his own conversions – leaving many converts relieved and many other "untrusted" rabbis scratching their heads in astonishment.

This series of events highlights one of the greatest paradoxes in Jewish life today. On the one hand, values of civil society seem to be regressing in some areas of Jewish life – particularly

What Will American Jewry Look Like in 10 years?

Orthodoxy, which enables and, in many cases, systematically perpetuates some awful abuses against women, converts and non-Orthodox Jews generally, both via the Israeli rabbinate and via the obstinately and anachronistically patriarchal RCA structure. To be sure, not all rabbis are Freundel. However, one needs to look no further than the infuriating situation of agunot – women chained in unwanted marriages – and the exasperating obstinacy of the all-male Orthodox rabbinical establishment to any suggestion of change to understand how deep the abuse of women is in Orthodoxy. Moreover, the Freundel story reminds us of how much Orthodox leadership remains a men's club: the RCA apparently received complaints from women about him, but chose to dismiss the complaints because, at the end of the day, Orthodox rabbis identified with the (male rabbinic) perpetrator more than with the (female, converting, powerless) victim. The depth of the gender problem in Orthodoxy is alarming on many levels.

On the other hand, there are some fascinating and even exciting advances for women across denominations, even Orthodoxy. Women in rabbinical leadership positions are a new reality, even if all denominations have work to do to claim real gender equality in leadership. The language of gender equality has infused many aspects of Jewish life, even if the yawning gender parity in pay and status in communal life has not improved much on the ground, according to four years of research by *The Forward*. Still, communal-wide discussion of once fraught issues such as homosexuality and sexual abuse are no longer taboo. The Jewish community, it seems, is working hard to move gender issues forward, while in some ways it seems to be moving backwards at the same time.

Sexual abuse epitomizes the paradox. Community-wide public discourse about the issue is clearly on the rise, along with the creation of Jewish organizations around the world to combat the issue. Jewish Community Watch hosts a "Wall of Shame" for suspected abusers, and hotlines for victims are being set up around the world, even special hotlines for men. However, if reporting and awareness are on the rise, it may also indicate that incidents of abuse are on the rise as well. Debbie Gross, founding director of the Crisis Center for Religious Women that recently hosted the first international conference on abuse in the Jewish community, often speaks about abuse as a growing epidemic. But it is very hard to know. Is abuse spreading or are we just hearing about it more? The answers to these questions remain unclear. It seems possible that both the problem and the solutions are simultaneously on the rise.

What Will American Jewry Look Like in 10 years?

The impression that the Jewish community is moving in two negating parallel processes comes from an examination of gender issues around the Jewish world. In my book, *The War on Women in Israel: A Story of Religious Radicalism and the Women Fighting for Freedom*, I document the many frightening ways in which radical Orthodoxy has been growing and taking ownership of women's lives and bodies – e.g., demands for gender segregation in public spaces; erasure of women's faces and bodies; silencing of women's voices, and more. Make no mistake: this is new. Twenty and thirty years ago, women sang and danced in public, Orthodox men freely sat next to women on buses, and even haredi (ultra-Orthodox) newspapers ran ads for women's hosiery without incident. Religious radicalism reached new intensity – and not only in Israel. The New York City Mayor's office has been intervening to try and stop the B110 bus line from imposing gender segregation. Barclay's Stadium holds gender segregated and men-only events. Signs on some streets in Brooklyn tell women that they are not welcome to stand there or dress a certain way. And of course the El Al planes, now notorious for allowing the oppression of women by radicals, are a key space where American and Israeli radicalism coalesce. The segregation takes place in Hebrew and English.

When it comes to Jewish radicalism, there is a noticeable cross-pollination between Israel and America.

Yet within all this, there is also a growing feminist movement throughout Israel and America, and in fact the Orthodox feminist movement is in some ways the most vocal. Social anthropologist Prof Tamar El Or, who has studied religious women's identities, argues that religious feminism is a more robust movement than secular feminism because, in religious life, the signs of patriarchy are so easily apparent. It's easier for a religious woman to grab hold of the symbols of sexism – e.g., holding a Torah on Simchat Torah (Jewish holiday marking the end of the annual Torah reading cycle) – because they are more glaring and less subtle than the sexism in the secular world. Certainly, there are fascinating signs of feminist change throughout the Jewish world and Orthodoxy. There is even a new haredi women's feminist movement that was formed last year during the municipal elections in Israel.

Still, signs are clear that Jewish life around the world faces growing radicalism. Judaism is not much different from the rest of the world in this respect. Pretty much all major religions have faced growing radicalism over the past 20 years, a radicalism that takes hold of women's bodies with violence and rage. Ultra-Orthodoxy is comparable to the Taliban, the Tea

What Will American Jewry Look Like in 10 years?

Party, and ISIS in this regard: they all believe that the path to God is through violent control of women's bodies.

Perhaps religious radicalism and feminism feed off of each other on some level. Already in the 1980s, Susan Faludi wrote her epic work, *Backlash*, about the anti-feminist, often religious-based backlash against women in America. The feminist movement has made tremendous gains since the publication of her book, and yet the very radicalism that she describes is getting worse. It is literally a war between forces of religious oppression and forces of women's freedom. And it is taking place in the Jewish world right now with increasing intensity.

Social media has also changed the dynamics of this war. The internet enables faster and fiercer fighting, with new tools that can literally kill. The internet is both a system for promoting grass-roots change and a dangerous weapon in the hands of the masses. The internet has been tremendous in advancing social movements through videos, blogs, and rapidly spreading hashtags. At the same time, online bullying has reached frightening heights, as the phenomenon of Facebook suicides spreads. Religious radicalism spreads this way too, even in the haredi world, through the spread of materials designed to fight the battle. Feminism spreads this way, as well, and, as leading feminist blogger

Rebecca Traister recently wrote, the internet has energized the feminist movement in exciting ways. Although the *New York Times* has published a series of articles suggesting that people do not really change their ideas much via social media and that Facebook is often more like a million little echo chambers for people to reinforce their own ideas, I think that, if we take a step back, we will see that this isn't entirely true. Social media has changed the dynamic of all of our lives, and we are all exposed to everything all the time. I agree with Rebecca Traister. Social media is in some ways a scary tool in the hands of violent radicals. But it also has the potential to empower revolutionaries. It has, without a doubt, a central place in the process of social change within Jewish life as well.

So where does all this leave the Jewish people? It is very hard to try and envision the next ten years – knowing, as we do, that we cannot possibly predict the impact of world events and technological advances; after all, put in perspective, a little more than ten years ago, there was no such thing as smartphones, Youtube, Facebook or Twitter. Still, it seems to me that we can take a look at some of the key trends that are going on today and see what would happen if they continue. And we can ask ourselves what our roles are in creating a world that we want to live in.

This is what I see: The Jewish people

What Will American Jewry Look Like in 10 years?

are experiencing two competing trends, pulling the community into two vastly different directions. One is based on a vision of dialogue with contemporary life and all its values, and one is based on a fundamentalist separatism and the oppression of women. The battle between these two forces takes place most often on women's bodies, as religious radical leaders use pressure about so-called "modesty" and the control of women's bodies to take charge of their flocks.

I believe that the primary goal of the Jewish community must be to fend off the spread of radicalism. This is not just for women, although women are the ones whose lives in some places are at real risk from violence. It is for the community itself, for the entire Jewish people, to preserve the diversity and dialogue that keeps Judaism alive.

The ones who are fighting the most to stave off radicalism are Jewish feminist activists. The community must find ways to support and empower the feminist movement, which I believe is currently the most important movement for the survival of the Jewish community. Jewish feminists are literally saving the Jewish people from the dangerous spread of radicalism. In Israel, the current elections are a battlefield over the place of religious radicalism in civil society. Even in the recent

election, just two years ago, Israelis flocked to parties like Yesh Atid that promised a future without religious radicalism. The most significant movement here is the growth of the fledgling haredi feminist movement, which is in the key position to halt the spread of radicalism. And the radicals know it as well. The fact that the all-male Shas party created a "women's committee" demonstrates that they know that their biggest threat right now is the revolution of women.

The feminist movement is the most important movement for fighting off religious radicalism in the Jewish world. The Jewish community must

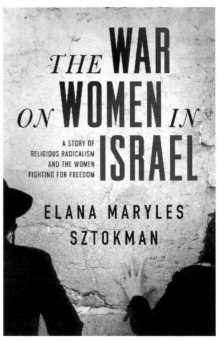

THE WAR ON WOMEN IN ISRAEL

A STORY OF RELIGIOUS RADICALISM AND THE WOMEN FIGHTING FOR FREEDOM

ELANA MARYLES SZTOKMAN

What Will American Jewry Look Like in 10 years?

support these women with all its might.

In ten years' time, the community will be headed in one of two directions: Either it will be a majority of haredim, ultra-Orthodox, whose male leaders will continue to pull communal discourse towards retrograde gender practices that oppress women and other living creatures, or the radicalism will have waned to a small minority as Orthodox women have staved off the radicalism and created real change from within. Whether or not the Jewish feminist movement will win depends in part on how much support they get from the larger Jewish community. It depends how much of the communal resources are used to support the Jewish feminist movement. The more resources are dedicated to supporting Jewish feminist women, the better the future will be for all of us.

Touro and the Ladder of the Jewish Future

Alan Kadish

➤ **Dr. Alan Kadish** is the President of the Touro College and University System.

In Genesis 28:10-19, Jacob falls asleep on a pile of stones while fleeing from his brother, Esau. Cast out of his home, in search of a future and in fear for his life, an exhausted Jacob stops to sleep at nightfall and dreams of a ladder on which angels ascend to heaven and descend to earth. In this dream, God tells Jacob about a future in which his descendants are prosperous and blessed by the nations of the world. In this encounter with God, with the promise of destiny in a time of fear and doubt, the image of the ladder stands as a symbol for the Jewish future.

A homiletic interpretation of this enigmatic dream is offered in the midrashic work, Chapters of Rabbi Eliezer. The upward and downward movements of the angels represent the rise and fall of the great civilizations in history. This interpretation charts the years of Babylon, Greece and Rome, among others, as rungs along the ladder of time, yet the Jewish nation is noticeably missing from the list of nations in the midrash. While it might be easier to understand the midrash to be relegating the Jewish people, as represented by Jacob, to be passive witnesses to history, I believe the absence of the Jewish people's angelic representative on the ladder to be a statement that denies a linear trajectory for the destiny of Judaism. I would like to think that describing the Jewish future in all its complexity was challenging even for our sages to do through midrash, so I hope that you will grant me leeway in my own attempt to provide a vision for the future of our people.

In the span of a 3,500 year old religion, ten years does not seem like enough time to measure significant change. In the greater context of the history of the Jewish people, the degree to which Judaism has changed since the beginning of 2005 to today is a question of minutiae instead of one of transformation. It would be easy to suggest that the same could be said about the next ten years; however, there are some reasons to believe that

➤ Touro and the Ladder of the Jewish Future

we may be entering an inflection point. In the past, as well as today, the many denominations of Judaism are striving to maintain relevance in an evolving world. They continue investing in continuity campaigns, battling anti-Semitism, and working diligently to support Jews in Israel and abroad in every conceivable way. The major threats to Judaism are far from new; crisis in the Middle East, alarming assimilation rates, and internal infighting and scandal are a few of the many important issues that have persisted throughout modernity.

However, in light of the accelerating rate of change on the international stage, with increasing economic instability, changing demographics and borders, and the actions of powder-keg figures and religious movements, it seems like tomorrow's newspaper headline always carries the potential to transform the trajectory of our lives. Climate change, ISIS, a nuclear Iran threatening the world with nuclear terrorism, and the fate of billions of lives subject to the shifting political realities across Eurasia are only some of the potential catalysts of which we are aware that can bring extreme world change.

While there are those that say that Judaism will look dramatically different in ten years from now, especially when considering how tumultuous our world looks, it is more productive when considering the glacial mass

of Jewish history to think about how an eternal people can stay ahistorical and contemporaneous in a constantly changing world. Without having the blessing of open revelation today, we must look to history as our guide in estimating the future needs of the Jewish people. However, such a perspective must be qualified by the recognition that, while much has been done and much continues to be done in an attempt to improve the prospective Jewish future, no one can definitively indicate which initiatives will have a significant impact and which will fade away. To paraphrase Rabbi Tarfon in the Ethics of the Fathers, it may not be in our power to complete the work, but we must not forsake it.

Touro College is the largest institution of higher education under Jewish auspices in the world; I, as President, recognize the gravity and the responsibility of asking, "Where do we want Judaism to be in ten years?" In ten years from now, I want to see many more, well-educated and engaged Jews, who are proud and passionate about their homeland, and who are working to create a more compassionate world. Those future Jews will need a foundation upon which to stand, one that we must build today. That foundation will need the components of a strong education that focuses on literacy of the Jewish heritage and not only on strong job and career preparation. It also demands a

Touro and the Ladder of the Jewish Future

grounded understanding of the world and the diversity of its inhabitants.

I envision a Judaism in which Jewish literacy has skyrocketed. According to last year's Pew study, only half of Jews (52%), say they know the Hebrew alphabet, but far fewer (13%) say they understand most or all of the words when they read Hebrew. The Jewish intellectual tradition is rooted in our texts, in the Torah, in the Talmud, and in thousands of years' worth of commentary. The fact that only about thirteen percent of Jews have access to the texts of their birthright without the aid of an intermediary, or translation, is disheartening to me as an educator and as a Jew who is in awe of the richness of our Jewish heritage.

Touro's undergraduate schools, i.e. the Lander Colleges in Manhattan and Queens and Touro College Los Angeles, have Jewish studies built into the core curriculum, and we currently educate thousands of students per year, giving them the tools to learn and teach others about our rich tradition. At Touro, we strive to educate beyond the classroom and reach the communities in which our schools are based. We host numerous lecture series throughout the year on topics ranging from biomedical ethics to the Jewish legal perspective on information privacy; we take every opportunity to share our educational resources in order to motivate and spread a passion for what the Jewish

intellectual tradition has to offer.

I envision a future in which all Jews are gainfully employed and feel empowered by their professional expertise and are stable enough in their lives to devote significant time and energy to their families and their religion. However, with the rising rate of inflation against the mostly stagnant median salary and expected income, the costs of keeping a kosher home and sending children to private religious schools seem out of reach for many people. We must prepare our children with the best professional training available.

Earning advanced degrees has a demonstrable and significant impact on lifelong income, and providing access to higher education must be a communal imperative in order for the Jewish future to continue to flourish. Thankfully, Judaism has always emphasized the importance of education, and that has almost certainly contributed to our resiliency and success as a people. However, as more and more Jews are concerned about the educational environments of secular schools, we need to provide a learning environment in which all Jews can feel comfortable and empowered to succeed.

At Touro, we prioritize our responsibilities to prepare our students to successfully navigate the challenges of the workplace, including maintaining a healthy work-life balance. While work-

Touro and the Ladder of the Jewish Future

life balance issues concern everybody, they can feel more demanding for Orthodox Jews struggling to meet the needs of work, family, community, and religious responsibility. Our response to this challenge is to utilize our extensive network of diverse graduate programs to offer innovative multidisciplinary programs and courses to our students. The integrated health science program, medical pathways program, and many research opportunities for our undergraduate students at our graduate schools give our students a strong competitive edge in the workplace. Superior education and preparation will enable our students to thrive in the workplace and empower them to live full, religiously devoted lives.

I envision a future in which Jews are not only passionate supporters of Israel, but educated advocates of Israel as well. Every Jewish person shares a stake in the land of Israel, and we need to bolster that claim with intellectual honesty and knowledge of Israel's history in a global context. While the complexity of Israel's situation can hardly be reduced to a position either for or against the country, a premise which is laughable in the context of any other country, discussions about Israel seem to take that approach. We cannot let divisive, ignorant ranting control our politics.

In many places where blatant anti-Semitism is no longer tolerated, anti-Israel rhetoric has taken its place as an accepted target for the same sentiment. That is not to imply that Israel is a perfect nation. I believe that Israel is governed by well-intentioned people of a high moral caliber; however they are placed in a difficult situation and must make difficult decisions. I may not agree with every decision made by the Israeli government, nor would I support every Israeli organization; however that doesn't mean that I can keep quiet while Israel, as a whole, and the Jewish people, by proxy, are condemned.

As part of his or her education, every Touro student must take core political science courses to prepare him or her with the basic understanding and language of global politics. In addition, we offer supplementary education in the form of community lectures and symposia on Israel to help elucidate the history and contemporary issues at hand in the region. With the skills and knowledge from a Touro education, our students are able to speak out in support of a nuanced understanding of the complexity of the conflicts in the Middle East. In ten years, there will be many more voices educated in our college system to lend their strength in support of reason and understanding with regard to Israel and its neighbors.

Finally, I envision a future in which all Jewish people love and respect one another. However, political infighting

Touro and the Ladder of the Jewish Future

and resentment is as old as the stories of the Torah. The rivalry between brothers starts with the first two siblings mentioned in the Torah, Cain and Abel. That literary thread is woven through Isaac and Ishmael, Jacob and Esau, and is manifest in the struggle between Yosef and his brothers. While that does not justify the internal tensions within the Jewish community, it emphasizes the tenacity of this problem.

In the next ten years, however, the challenges of unifying the various segments of the global Jewish community will come to a head. Fault lines are forming over the issues of Israel advocacy and religious observance. Controversy on college campuses regarding certain Hillel groups promoting anti-Zionist speakers, controversy on J-street's place within the Conference of Presidents, and controversy regarding what constitutes effective Israel advocacy in general is fracturing our community into distinct factions. With the growing Hasidic and Yeshivish communities and the widening of Orthodox Judaism to include a broader range of perspectives, the confusion created by the blurring boundaries of religious observance has been fueling reactionary attitudes on inter-communal conversation within the Jewish community. In attempts to distinguish one sect from another, we are creating divisive fences, instead of open doorways for communication.

While Touro, as an institution of higher education, will not become embroiled in communal or religious politics, we are in a unique position to help build bridges between disparate Jewish communities. As a link between the neighborhoods in which our schools are based, with programs in Israel, Moscow, Berlin, and Paris as well as across the United States, Touro can provide the events, gatherings, and general umbrella under which many Jews can find common ground. It is my hope that Touro will continue to be a welcoming home and a place of friendship for all Jewish people.

In our mission, it states that we were established to perpetuate and enrich the Jewish heritage and to support Jewish continuity, as well as to serve the general community in keeping with the historic Jewish commitment to the transmission of knowledge, social justice, and compassionate concern for, and service to, society. Touro does not

➤ Touro and the Ladder of the Jewish Future

simply accommodate Jewish traditions, it supports and sustains them. The College is one of few in this country that ensures opportunities for students to worship and to study, to celebrate and to honor their cultures and beliefs. I believe Touro is uniquely positioned as the largest institution under Jewish auspices to deliver this vision of a better prepared and educated Jewish people who together will forge a bright and prosperous Jewish future.

Our answer is to connect and educate all members of the Jewish community, whether in our classrooms or at our community-wide events. We don't ask people their religious or political opinions before they join our conversations or before we include them within the context of our mission. In the next ten years, Touro will strive to continue to cultivate a culturally sensitive environment of respect in which all engaged members of the Jewish community can communicate and relate to one another, while providing the broader world with a model of excellence towards which to aspire.

Knowing and Owning our Story: Sustaining the Jewish Future

Richard Joel

➤ **President Richard Joel** *is the President of Yeshiva University.*

We are a people of history, but also one of destiny. Our history serves as the foundation for our continued growth, but we must feel a sense of ownership over our observance and community to create a sustainable future and to become the people we aspire to be. We also must recognize that our "siloed" communities are moving towards extremes in opposite directions, and a big tent of American Jewry is getting harder and harder to pitch. From Yeshiva University's point of view, we have an obligation to provoke the leadership of our young people who embrace a Jewish value system and lifestyle, are involved in Torah study, and feel a sense of Kol Yisrael Areivim Zeh B'Zeh, that every Jew is responsible for one another.

Jewish life, and our value system, will not transmit by osmosis. Spirituality and closeness to God is not something we feel because it is the way that our parents and grandparents felt. Jews today choose Judaism and, therefore, need to both know and own the Jewish narrative to develop a meaningful connection to Jewish life. Thankfully, the Modern Orthodox day school system has produced literate, knowing Jews. But Judaism is much richer than mere Torah knowledge; it infuses a sense of passion and spirit into everyday life. As educators, we must ask ourselves, are we presenting Judaism as vital and vibrant enough to resonate with our students? Are we transmitting ideas and practices in a way that is meaningful enough to matter? At Hillel, I often spoke of the goal of "maximizing the number of Jews doing Jewish." And, "doing Jewish," being fired up by rituals so integral to the Jewish experience, is crucial for the American Jewish community that seeks a sustainable future.

At Yeshiva University, we are looking towards the notion of an integrated community that inspires a sense of wholeness in its students, an aspiration for wholeness within the

Knowing and Owning our Story: Sustaining the Jewish Future

community. More and more of the lay and professional Jewish leadership positions will be filled by people who are passionate about this notion. For these reasons, we are offering more certificates and training programs for Jewish professionals that will enhance and professionalize our leadership. Experiential Jewish education must be content and value-driven, delivered through experiences that enable learners to authentically experience, reflect, conceptualize, and experiment with what they have learned. For example, the objective of our certificate program for Experiential Jewish Education is "the deliberate infusion of Jewish values and content into engaging and memorable experiences that impact the formation of Jewish identity." We offer a certificate for Jewish Philanthropy that works in tandem with the Wurzweiler School of Social Work to train and enable the next generation of professionals to confront fundraising challenges within the Jewish world and nonprofits. Our service-learning missions send undergraduates across the country and around the world to directly engage and volunteer on a global level. Programs such as these are expected to produce a cohort of lay leaders and professionals that, in turn, will inspire a renewed engagement with the Jewish experience.

A bright future lies ahead. Through enabling an invigorated leadership to inspire passionate participation and rebuilding the community with a sense of wholeness, we can achieve.

Modern Orthodoxy, Whither?

Elana Stein Hain

➤ **Dr. Elana Stein Hain** *is the Director of Leadership Education at the Shalom Hartman Institute of North America. She holds a doctorate in Religion from Columbia University, and she served as clergy at Lincoln Square Synagogue and the Jewish Center. She lives on the Upper West Side with her husband Rabbi Yonah Hain and her sons Azzan and Navon.*

Judaism has known its fair share of schism. Schism is defined as a formal division within, or a separation from, a religious body over some doctrinal difference. To offer a few "highlights": the Sadducees and Pharisees of the Second Temple Period, the Karaites and the Rabbinites in the eighth century, 17th century Sabbateanism, Denominationalism in the nineteenth century, etc. But there is also something less divisive than schism to which Judaism is no stranger either: debate. According to Professor Shaye Cohen, the Mishnah was our first Jewish document to record debate without assuming schism to be the ultimate result (from "The Significance of Yavneh: Pharisees, Rabbis, and the End of Jewish Sectarianism"), and debate has existed throughout our history without hint of schism. Rabbinic law is, in fact, built on healthy argumentation. So, what distinguishes between debating factions and ultimately schismatic sects?

Before delving too deeply into this question, I should say at the outset that my goal is to discuss the future of Modern Orthodoxy, specifically in North America. Upon its birth in the nineteenth century, Modern Orthodoxy, or neo-Orthodoxy as it was known, presented itself as the response to full integration into secular European society. An emancipated (or nearly so) Western European Jewry found itself able to envision for the first time in a long time different possibilities for Jewish living within secular culture, and so the discussions began. With the birth of the Reform movement, itself a response to Jewish emancipation, Samson Raphael Hirsch decided that he too would offer his own religious response to modernity over and against that of his former university classmate, Abraham Geiger. Yet even though Hirsch is credited as the founder of Modern Orthodoxy, neo-Orthodoxy was never monolithic. In fact, its leadership and its adherents were divided between the Hirschian camp, whose understanding of

Modern Orthodoxy, Whither?

Torah im Derekh Eretz was for the purpose of being a Mensch-Jisroel, and the Hildesheimer camp, which embraced Wissenschaft des Judentums (essentially, a historicized study of Judaism as opposed to a more timeless and decontextualized understanding of the development of Judaism in its various iterations). These two positions were indicative of varying stances regarding the relationship between Judaism and the secular world. Nevertheless, neo-Orthodoxy remained a single denomination, despite its internal tensions and even vituperative rhetoric. Perhaps it is because, ultimately, the two subgroups had more in common than they had dividing them.

Today, it seems that Orthodoxy is on the precipice of true schism between what might be deemed the evolution of the Hirschian and the Hildesheimer camps, the former known today as Modern Orthodoxy and the latter now known as Open Orthodoxy. To be sure, the term Open Orthodoxy is overused (and often used simply as a moniker for Jews who embrace a liberal lifestyle but still affiliate with Orthodoxy). Nonetheless, this tagline for the founding of Yeshivat Chovevei Torah (YCT) over a decade ago, is arguably the heir to Hildesheimer's brand of neo-Orthodoxy. On the other side of the coin, Yeshiva University's representation of Modern Orthodoxy

bears similarity to Hirsch's. This is not to say that either of today's neo-Orthodox camps lines up perfectly with either Hildesheimer or Hirsch; in fact, both nineteenth-century figures were likely too conservative on the issue of secular education and its integration with Torah study for either group to adopt its predecessor wholeheartedly. Some may argue, however, that the fear of schism is overwrought. Today's subdivisions of neo-Orthodoxy have much overlap between them. Members of the Rabbinical Council of America include rabbis who affiliate with Open Orthodoxy, and the International Rabbinic Fellowship include those who received their semicha at Yeshiva University. While some of this is due simply to the fact that YCT was founded rather recently, it is also because there are religious leaders who truly relate to both sub-movements in some fundamental way.

Another point of potential schism relates to the role of Orthodox women. While the history of Jewish movements is often the history of male leadership, the place of women in this impending rift is fundamental. There are three major training programs in North America for female religious leadership in the neo-Orthodox community (listed in order of their founding): Nishmat's Yoetzet Halacha Program, Yeshiva University's Graduate Program in Advanced Talmudic Studies (GPATS),

Modern Orthodoxy, Whither?

and Yeshivat Maharat. While each of these programs seems to be carving out its own political, social and religious niche, it is quite telling that all are moving forward quite successfully at the same time. This general success of all the programs marks a groundswell of change taking place within North American neo-Orthodoxy, which arguably differs more in how women should play a leadership role than in recognizing the need and the value of female leadership. (Just to note, Dr. Jennie Rosenfeld has recently been appointed to a communal religious leadership role in Efrat, which pushes me at least to note how much more can be written on this topic with regards to Israel!)

Similarities aside, Modern and Open Orthodoxy vehemently avow their distinctions from one another. They have separate councils for giyur (conversion) and for Jewish divorce, and affiliated synagogues will hire exclusively from YCT/Maharat or REITS/GPATS. This speaks to more than mere diversity. It bespeaks ideological divisions. Those divisions revolve mostly around pluralism and gender, two topics that have been definitive for neo-Orthodoxy since the 1950s as part of the ideological battles between Orthodox and Conservative Judaism. To illustrate, the installment of Rabbi Asher Lopatin as President of YCT sparked a roundtable

discussion of rabbis representing diverse denominations over YCT and Orthodox Judaism. Similarly, following the ordination of Rabba Sara Hurwitz, the Rabbinical Council of America issued a statement supporting female religious leadership while rejecting rabbinical roles for women. Certainly, these discussions were over more than technical disparities; they demonstrate major ideological and adaptive differences between Modern and Open Orthodoxy. They also reflect two different views about the emphasis on Jewish Peoplehood, as well as on the nature of religious truth and the evolution of halakhah. Make no mistake, these foundational questions impact what is often deemed "technical" halakhic discourse, such as policies and standards for conversion, kashrut standards, etc.

This diverging of neo-Orthodoxy is not only at the level of leadership. The laity, too, is deeply divided in certain ways and deeply united in others. The areas of diversity that I see emerging from the laity relate to partnership-minyanim and political leanings. While there was once an understanding that an Orthodox service would not include female ritual leadership, many lay-initiated minyanim exist that do. Partnership-minyanim are the subject of conversation in synagogues, around Shabbat tables, and on college campuses. They give many within

Modern Orthodoxy, Whither?

neo-Orthodoxy a place to pray, while others see them as a source of true alienation from certain segments that are otherwise rather similar. Regarding politics, while Orthodox Jewry is thought to be overwhelmingly republican and center-right on issues relating to Israel, anecdotal evidence indicates that there is more diversity of opinion, especially among younger Orthodox Jews, than the Pew Report can capture.

The question today is, where is neo-Orthodoxy, whether it be Modern or Open Orthodoxy going? Is a rift a good idea, as many rifts have been before, or is it a bad idea? I would like to look at two models of decision-making and consensus building in the Talmud in order to discuss the parameters of this question.

The first model is based on the commandment of lo tasur: thou shall not deviate. (See Deuteronomy 17:8-13.) The context is judicial: the Supreme Court in Jerusalem rules. Its decision is law, period. There is no option for deviation. After all, this will ensure the stability of any and all rulings. Even a member of that very Supreme Court who had the dissenting opinion must follow the ultimate ruling of the court, and if he deviates he becomes what is known as a zaqen mamre, a "rebellious elder." It is clear that this perspective leads easily to sectarianism. If there is only one way to do things, and it must

be heeded by all, one who deviates is no longer part of the group. While there are certain bright red lines within neo-Orthodoxy in North America, this notion is really not the prevailing tenor of the conversation. Neo-Orthodox communities and leaders seek to include rather than cast out.

A more appropriate paradigm is the one that was instituted when the Jewish people no longer had an ability to enforce its norms through government and had experienced plenty of schism – namely at the founding of Yavneh, the religious enclave which birthed the Mishnah. It was during this time that active debate which did not result in schism was developed. As Jewish historian Shaye Cohen points out, the Mishnah was the first document to record disparate opinions and their advocates by name. It could hold different viewpoints together. What kept this from becoming too diffuse was as spirit of lo titgodedu, a clause in the Bible parsed by rabbinic homiletics as "do not become fractious." (See Sifre Re'eh Paragraph 96 based on Deuteronomy 14:1.)

The Jerusalem Talmud seems to indicate that this strategy of debate within a unified community resulted in relatively uniform behavior even in the realm of custom where diversity has always been most rampant (See JT Pesahim 4:1). The Babylonian Talmud, however, edited at least a century after

Modern Orthodoxy, Whither?

the Jerusalem Talmud, tells perhaps a more practical story of how lo titgodedu might work in practice:

Abaye said: When we apply, 'lo titgodedu,' we refer to a situation such as having two courts in one city, one which rules like the House of Shammai and the other like the house of Hillel, but two courts in two different cities is not problematic. Rava said to him: But were not the Houses of Shammai and Hillel themselves similar to having two courts in one city? Rather, Rava said: When we apply, 'lo titgodedu,' we refer to a situation such as having one court in a city in which half the decisors rule like the House of Shammai and half rule like the House of Hillel. But having two courts [which rule differently] in a single city is not problematic. (Babylonian Talmud Yevamot 14a)

This model seems much more akin to the type of Judaism that we have in North America, as well as the type of neo-Orthodoxy that we see: there clearly are debates, and there clearly is not (full) uniformity in practice, but there still are ways in which practice clusters around different places. Rava's perspective, however, pushes the envelope more than Abaye's position: His concern seems primarily for each court to be able to set its own norms. When that ability is hindered, and thus no ultimate policy is made, it is problematic.

Where does this leave us in regards to either Modern or Open Orthodoxy? Perhaps it offers a positive model for thoroughgoing debate without the necessity for schism. While Rava's is an expensive option in terms of fundraising and the like, it is probably the most welcome option for a denomination that is small enough not to be interested in further schism.

Investing In The Future

Rabbi Lord Jonathan Sacks

> **Rabbi Lord Jonathan Sacks** *is a global religious leader, philosopher, author and moral voice for our time. He is currently the Ingeborg and Ira Rennert Global Distinguished Professor of Judaic Thought at New York University and the Kressel and Ephrat Family University Professor of Jewish Thought at Yeshiva University. He has also been appointed as Professor of Law, Ethics and the Bible at King's College London. Previously, Rabbi Sacks served as Chief Rabbi of the United Hebrew Congregations of the Commonwealth between September 1991 and September 2013, only the sixth incumbent since the role was formalized in 1845.*

In Parshat Matot, the Israelites are almost within sight of the Promised Land. They have waged a victorious campaign against the Midianites. We feel the tempo quicken. No longer are the Israelites in the desert. They are moving inexorably toward the Jordan, to the west of which lies their destination: the land 'flowing with milk and honey'.

The members of the tribes of Reuben and Gad, though, begin to have different thoughts. Seeing that the land through which they are travelling is ideal for raising cattle, they decide that they would like to stay there, to the east of the Jordan. Moses is angry at the suggestion:

Moses said to the Gadites and Reubenites, "Shall your countrymen go to war while you sit here? Why do you discourage the Israelites from going over into the land the Lord has given them?"

The tribes meet his objection with a compromise formula:

Then they came up to him and said, "We would like to build pens here for our livestock and cities for our women and children. But we are ready to arm ourselves and go ahead of the Israelites until we have brought them to their place. Meanwhile our women and children will live in fortified cities, for protection from the inhabitants of the land. We will not return to our homes until every Israelite has received his inheritance. We will not receive any inheritance with them on the other side of the Jordan, because our inheritance has come to us on the east side of the Jordan."

We are willing, they tell Moses, to join the rest of the Israelites in the battles that lie ahead. Indeed we are willing to go on ahead, to be the advance guard, to be in the forefront of the battle. It is not that we are afraid of battle. Nor are

➤ Investing In The Future

we trying to evade our responsibilities toward our people as a whole. It is simply that we wish to raise cattle, and this land to the east of the Jordan is ideal. Warning them of the seriousness of their undertaking, Moses agrees. If they keep their word, they may settle east of the Jordan.

That is the story on the surface. But as so often in the Torah, there are subtexts as well as texts. One in particular was noticed by the sages, with their sensitivity to nuance and detail. Listen carefully to what the Reubenites and Gadites said:

Then they came up to him and said, "We would like to build pens here for our livestock and cities for our women and children."

Moses replies:

"Build cities for your children, and pens for your flocks, but do what you have promised."

The ordering of the nouns is crucial. The men of Reuben and Gad put property before people: they speak of their flocks first, their women and children second. Moses reverses the order, putting special emphasis on the children. As Rashi notes:

"They paid more regard to their property than to their sons and daughters, because they mentioned their cattle before the children. Moses said to them: 'Not so. Make the main thing primary and the subordinate thing secondary. First build cities for

your children, and only then, folds for your flocks.'"

The midrash (Bamidbar Rabbah 22:9) makes the same point through a dazzling interpretation of the line in Ecclesiastes: "The heart of the wise inclines to the right, but the heart of the fool to the left." (Ecclesiastes 10:2) The midrash identifies 'right' with Torah and life: "He brought the fire of a religion to them from his right hand." (Deut. 33:2) 'Left' refers to worldly goods: "Long life is in her right hand; in her left hand are riches and honour." (Proverbs 3:16) The men of Reuben and Gad put 'riches and honour' before faith and posterity. Moses hints to them that their priorities are wrong. The midrash continues: The Holy One, blessed be He, said to them: "Seeing that you have shown greater love for your cattle than for human souls, by your life, there will be no blessing in it."

One of the most consistent patterns of Jewish history is the way communities through the ages put children and their education first. Already in the first century Josephus was able to write: "The result of our thorough education in our laws, from the very dawn of intelligence, is that they are, as it were, engraved on our souls." In twelfth century France a Christian scholar noted: "A Jew, however poor, if he has ten sons, will put them all to letters, not for gain as the Christians do, but for the understanding of G-d's law – and not

➤ Investing In The Future

only his sons but his daughters too."

In 1432, at the height of Christian persecution of Jews in Spain, a synod was convened at Valladolid to institute a system of taxation to fund Jewish education for all. In 1648, at the end of the Thirty Years' War, the first thing Jewish communities in Europe did to re-establish Jewish life was to re-organise the educational system. In their classic study of the shtetl, the small townships of Eastern Europe, Zborowski and Herzog write this about the typical Jewish family:

"The most important item in the family budget is the tuition fee that must be paid each term to the teacher of the younger boys' school. Parents will bend in the sky to educate their son. The mother, who has charge of household accounts, will cut the family food costs to the limit if necessary, in order to pay for her sons schooling. If the worst comes to the worst, she will pawn her cherished pearls in order to pay for the school term. The boy must study, the boy must become a good Jew – for her the two are synonymous."

In 1849, when Samson Raphael Hirsch became rabbi in Frankfurt, he insisted that the community create a school before building a synagogue. After the Holocaust, the few surviving yeshivah heads and Hassidic leaders concentrated on encouraging their followers to have children and build schools.

It is hard to think of any other religion or civilization that is as child-centred as Judaism, nor any that has predicated its very existence on putting their education first. There have been Jewish communities in the past that were affluent and built magnificent synagogues – Alexandria in the first centuries of the Common Era is an example. Yet because they did not put children first, they contributed little to the Jewish story. They flourished briefly, then disappeared.

Moses' implied rebuke to the tribes of Reuben and Gad is not a minor detail but a fundamental statement about Jewish priorities. Property is secondary, children primary.

Civilizations that value the young, stay young. Those that invest in the future, have a future. It is not what we own that gives us a share in eternity, but those to whom we give birth and the effort we make to ensure that they carry our belief and way of life into the next generation.

This article has been printed with the kind permission of The Office of RabbiSacks. To read more of Rabbi Lord Jonathan Sacks' work, including his weekly Covenant & Conversation parsha commentaries, or to subscribe to his mailing list, please visit www.rabbisacks.org or follow him on Twitter @RabbiSacks.

Made in the USA
Lexington, KY
10 February 2015